D1613043

THE TRAIL OF THE ARCTIC NOMADS

The Trail
of the
Arctic Nomads

HUGH BRANDON-COX

*Illustrated with colour
and black and white photographs by the Author*

WILLIAM KIMBER · LONDON

First published in 1969 by
WILLIAM KIMBER AND CO LTD
6 Queen Anne's Gate, London, SW1

© William Kimber & Co. Ltd, 1969
Standard Book Number 7183 0341 5

*This book is Copyright. No part of it may be
reproduced in any form without permission in
writing from the publishers except by a reviewer
who wishes to quote brief passages in connection
with a review written for inclusion in a newspaper or a radio broadcast.*

Printed in Great Britain by
W & J Mackay & Co Ltd, Chatham, Kent

Contents

Illustrations

8   *Illustrations*

Text Illustrations

Acknowledgements

This is a personal account of many months spent with the old Nomadic Lapp family of Sara, in the north of Norway. The large area of Lapland known as *Sameōednåm*, in which nomadic and settled Lapps, or *Same*, have lived for centuries, stretches from the White Sea in the north-east to Lake Femund in the south-west. In Finland there are no Lapps today south of the Saariselka ridge, but in Sweden they are as far south as Dalecarlia, and in Norway as far south as the Lake Femund, which is south of Røros. In the north and the west the region reaches to the Norwegian Sea and the Barents Sea.

The *Same* family of Sara is very old, and has followed the same migratory routes spring and autumn for a great many years. It was my intention to try to meet them, travel with them, and learn something of their culture and way of life.

In order to do this I had to have assistance from many sources, and here I would like to express my warm thanks to the Norwegian Travel Bureau in London, and to the Norwegian Embassy for their support and financial help.

My thanks are also due to Ørnulo Vorren and Ernst Manker, the joint authors of the excellent book *Lapp Life and Customs*, and to Peter Freuchen and Finn Salomonsen, the authors of *The Arctic Year*, for the help I received from their works. There has been a great amount of research into the cultural life of the Lapps, and a large number of books and papers have been written in the past. Among the best are Johannes Schefferus's *Lapponia*, from 1673, Knud Leem's *Beskrivelse over Finnmarkens Lapper* (An Account of the Finnmark Lapps), from 1767; and Gustav von Duden's *Om Lappland och Lapparne* (Lappland and the Lapps), from 1873.

Many museums have collections of Lapp articles, and on the Norwegian coast, the museum of Tromsø, founded in 1872, is of particular interest and importance.

Habits and customs can vary between groups that have adapted themselves to either a settled existence or who still follow the reindeer herds. It was my desire to write an account of the daily life over a long period of a typical nomadic family, and without the good-humoured support of the following Lapps the book could never have been written: Fru Ellen Christine Sara, Aslak, Nils and Anna Sara, Ole Gaino and Karin Gaino, Per Kemi, Marit, Mikkel and Ellen Kemi, and Ellen Sara, Berit and Hannah, my valuable and so willing helpers, and all the many children of the various families.

The north Norwegian fishing families could not have given me a better welcome in every home, and my thanks are due to them also.

But perhaps my warmest thanks are due to a member of our party who gave me moral support in so many ways . . . the hooded crow that I rescued when its nesting tree blew down in a spring storm. It was a symbol of the north that eventually followed me back to England.

The journey was an experience that very few foreigners can have had. It can never be forgotten, and it has had the most lasting impression on me in many ways. I can only hope that in the pages of my book some of the drama, difficulty, good humour and also pleasure of this ancient way of life become alive to the reader. As every page has been written, so have I relived each day; of calm and beauty; of biting winds and fierce storms; of being part of an ancient ritual.

The nomadic Lapps with whom I travelled will survive in their areas for many years ahead. They are now aided by a wise Norwegian Government, who have made conditions easier for them in a great many ways. It is my hope that they will continue to be found following the big herds of domesticated reindeer on this vast Finnmark Vidda in the north of Norway.

Cambridge and   HUGH BRANDON-COX
Sweden, 1969

CHAPTER I

The People of the White Wilderness

How and why did my immensely long and exciting journey begin? It was to a part of the world described in the sixth century by the Gothic historian, Jordanes, as: '. . . where there was snow both winter and summer, where the sun shone throughout the night in the middle of the summer, and where in the middle of the winter, the darkness of the night continued through the day. Strange the land and strange the people; they pursued the wild beasts on their magic pieces of wood, dressed in animal skins, looking like animals, and like animals eating raw meat.'

Probably because my father was an explorer, and both my mother and grandmother were also filled with the desire to travel and explore and probe into little-known places of the world, the urge had been born into me. Certainly I remember that all my presents as a boy were books of adventure, and at the earliest age I was often sent into the woods with a little food to cook for the day, and instructions to come back with a full report of everything I had seen. It was good training, and always at the back of my mind was the old book I had taken from the study at home and read about the north and its strange people.

Many years later, and after adventures in other parts of the world, I visited the Scott Polar Institute in Cambridge, my home, and in the quietness of the library I again became filled with the enthusiasm I had experienced as a small boy. The atmosphere of the library, with its deep ticking clock, lured me into a trance-like state as I pursued my studies, a little deeper, of these ancient people known as the Lapps, or *Samer*.

As I read I recalled the words of the old Lapp teacher, Isak Saba, as clearly as if he were sitting beside me and whispering into my ear . . .

'Far to the North, under the stars of the Great Bear, our Lapland silently looms:

'. . . glittering peaks and ancient grey ridges . . .

'. . . and the streams rush and the forests sigh . . .'

Sitting by a camp fire in the darkness of the night, I had read those words long ago. Then I had allowed my fantasy to carry me to the far north, to a people whose lives were still lived far from the rush and roar and stress of the modern world: a people who still travelled by sledge over long distances, and whose clothes were provided in great part by the reindeer whose tracks they must follow each spring and autumn.

In my father's old study were many maps. The study was now mine, but his personality still made me treat it with respect as though he was there. Unrolling his maps of the north I studied them with a new interest. The enthusiasm to travel to the land of the *Samer* was strong in me. It was near Christmas, and the shops were full of cards showing forests and snow and reindeer, as they have always done.

I sat in one of the old pubs in Cambridge. A friend came over to me and asked: 'Where are you off to next time? We should like a piece for the paper, you know.'

'You remember during the war all those lonely and cold patrols along the Norwegian coast?' I inquired.

'Yes . . .'

'Well, I'm going back up there as far as one can travel. I don't know how I shall do it, but I'm going to have a shot at meeting and living with one of these Lapp families.' With this I showed him the book I had been reading, and he glanced through the pages at some of the old engraved pictures, with growing interest.

'You're welcome to that lot. Rather you than me. I should have thought you had had enough during the war. I know I did. Anyway, it will make a good story. Tell me when you have fixed things up.'

We drank our beer, and I knew he thought I would forget all about it after Christmas. But he was mistaken. I contacted first the Norwegian National Travel Bureau in London, who were delighted, but knew really as little about this Arctic wilderness as I did. But they promised to contact Alta in the north of Norway, and try to locate someone there. The Norwegian Embassy shared my enthusiasm and said they would try to obtain a grant for me. My good friend Hugh Osgood of the Educational Foundation for Visual Aids was to provide me with all the colour film for the making of two films about the life of these people— if I ever got there!

When one wants seriously to go on such an expedition alone, one has to have a strong streak of persistence and worry people until one gets what one wants . . . or at least part of it. I worried the London offices until they managed to contact, through one of the Norwegian northern offices, a nomadic Lapp family called Sara who were one of the oldest in the north, and yet who they thought might take me with them, for payment, of course, on their long trail south with their reindeer to the summer grazing-grounds at the coast.

It appeared that one of the family, an unmarried daughter called Berit, had once been on a journey down to Oslo. A very long way it was for her indeed. One day, all dressed up in her very colourful best Lapp clothing, she had been admiring the Royal Palace. She had not been standing there long before a tall and dignified man had approached her and begun a conversation in Norwegian, which Berit could speak.

'Would you like to see over the Palace?' he had asked, and before she could understand completely what was happening she found herself inside the Royal Palace, with the Guard giving the royal salute. And to make the story complete, her host had been the Norwegian King himself, who had seen her from the Palace grounds, and had been fascinated by her clothing. She had been entertained, and indeed had made an appearance on the television when the story became known. So Berit had returned to her wilderness world of snow, reindeer, and sledges with a quite amazing story to tell.

It was because of this that she was known, and it was thought she and her family might be ready to have me. We would probably be able to speak together, as I had learned Swedish some time ago, and this is close to the Norwegian language. I felt I had a good chance to make myself understood, with her at any rate. The ancient Lappish tongue is immensely difficult for a foreigner, but I relied on the fact that Norwegian is being more spoken today amongst these Lapps, and especially the youngsters, who have to learn it at school.

It was a step in the right direction, but no one knew how they could contact the family. One could write a letter to the nearest little trading-post and it would wait there for one of the nomads to come out of the winter wilderness which is their home, and pick it up when he or she took fresh supplies of flour or sugar. That is what we decided to do. But I could not wait for any reply, for I knew from my studies that the ancient nomads in whose way of travel and life I had such a great interest, left for the spring migration to the coast, about the middle of April, and time was quickly passing.

Whilst I was awaiting various papers, I turned again to some of the many old books that had been written from the earliest days about this very old culture. It has fascinated scholars and historians from the time of the Roman, Tacitus, who described what he had heard of the Lapps, in A.D. 98. According to his accounts, there lived in the north a people who were entirely wild, being without horses or proper homes, and clad only in skins. They ate what they found growing wild, and only thin wood huts protected them from the cold and also the wild beasts. They were skilful with the use of bow and arrow, and the arrows they tipped with bone, as they had no iron. When they went hunting the wild animals their womenfolk went with them. These indeed must have been a very barbaric race.

Again in the sixth century a Byzantine writer told of a people of the strange land of Thule in the north, who were so wild that they drank no wine, could not cultivate the earth, and used sinews as thread to make clothing from skins. (This I was to see with my own eyes, which shows how little the ancient culture has changed in certain ways since those days.)

Later writers, always attracted by the remoteness and strangeness of the people of the cold Arctic regions, continued their chronicles in a similar manner, and it was in the thirteenth century that the big area became known as *Lappia* or Lapland, and the people, the Lapps. At the time of the Roman Tacitus, these Lapps had occupied the whole of the land we call Finland, but they then began to be pushed northwards as the Finns themselves started to populate and cultivate the country from the south. The Lapps, being hunters, were well able to survive, especially among the huge herds of wild reindeer. Long before, they had mastered the art of moving fast over the snow on skis, and their survival has depended greatly on this method of travel.

The home of the Lapps, or *Samer*, lies across a broad belt in the north of Norway, Sweden, Finland, and parts of Russia, and today there are roughly estimated to be about 35,000 of these people, of whom Norway

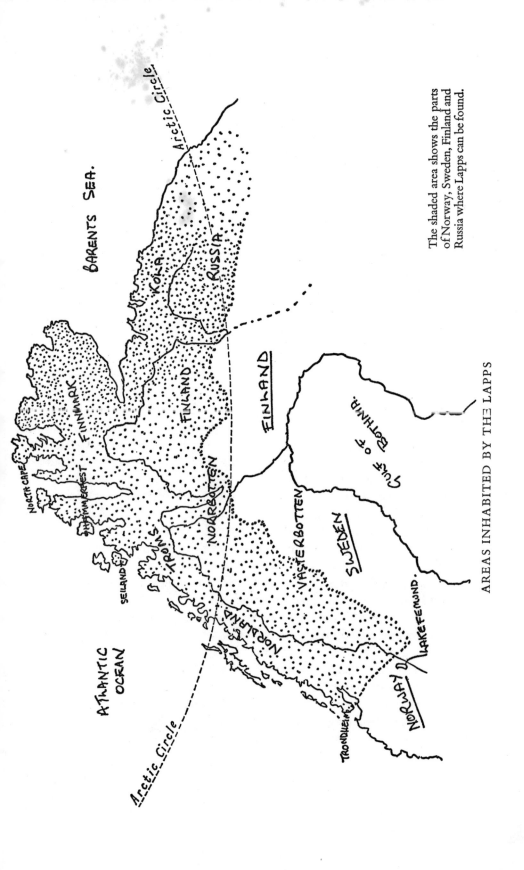

The shaded area shows the parts of Norway, Sweden, Finland and Russia where Lapps can be found.

AREAS INHABITED BY THE LAPPS

has by far the greatest number. There are perhaps more than 20,000 in Norway, which has two Lapp townships in the Finnmark region, called Karasjok and Kautokeino.

From the earliest times the Lapps, like other Arctic dwellers, depended upon the indigenous animals for their survival. These animals had been able to supply all their needs, not only for food but for clothing and even lighting as well. The sea also offered a wide variety of fish, and together with the reindeer, and the northern birds that added a variety to the diet, the essentials to maintain life had always been there.

There have been many theories about Lapp infiltration into Scandinavia. They wandered, it is thought, possibly from the east into their cold and at times harsh but beautiful world, several thousands of years ago. From the start of their life as we know it they lived as hunters, trappers and fishers. In many places along the rugged coast of Finnmark simple stone implements have been found that show people lived there as long as 8,000 years ago. Whether they were Lapps, however, is very difficult to know; but implements dating back some 4,000 years have been discovered that were certainly used by a people who lived by trapping and hunting the wild reindeer. These beasts roamed by the thousands over this vast area that knows only deep snow for many months of the year, and has short summers where there is no darkness and the plants and vegetation grow for the whole of the twenty-four hours of each day and night.

One very interesting account we have of early Lapp life comes from Ottar, a north Norwegian chief, who in 892 came to England and gave a report of his life to King Alfred. This old report is important because Ottar lived in the most northern region then occupied by the fierce Norsemen. North of him, however, were people who lived in small groups along the desolate lonely fjords, There they fished in summer and hunted the wild animals in winter for food and clothing materials.

Ottar related to Alfred his adventurous journey when he sailed north in one of the longships for three days and three nights, and then twelve days and nights to the north-east. He came to a very wide river, up which he was afraid to sail in case he was attacked. Until he reached that river he had seen no signs of humans. There, however, were people who we know as the Lapps, fishing along the banks, with the smoke rising from their wood fires.

We can well imagine this primitive scene, and Ottar continues his story to Alfred by saying that he himself was among the richest in his country. He farmed and had large herds of livestock. He received, he boasted, taxes from his Lapp neighbours in the form of reindeer and bear skins, feathers, whalebone, and even ropes made from the skins of seal and walrus.

He was the first to mention definitely that the Lapps had domesticated the reindeer, and he claimed himself to have a herd of some 600 beasts, of which six were the valuable decoy animals used by the Lapps as a lure to capture the wild reindeer.

It was not until the sixteenth century, however, that the Swede, Olaus Magnus, writing his history of the Scandinavian people, stated that the Lapps had developed into reindeer breeders, which meant that they were forced to become nomads, following in the wake of the animals which had the urge to migrate in the spring and autumn.

From the earliest times a hunting and fishing culture had existed, and gradually over the years the Lapps divided into various branches. Some became coast Lapps, living in fixed settlements along the coast and fishing for their main occupation. From their bases they made hunting expeditions in the mountains and forests, and fished in the lakes and the sea.

The reindeer herders and breeders, who have always been forced to move with their herds, which has given them no chance to become farmers in any way, also separated into two large groups. Some became mountain Lapps, whilst others, as with the old Lapp family of Sara with whom I was to travel, became a mixture of inland and coast Lapps, moving backwards and forwards with the changing seasons, year after year, generation after generation.

National frontiers made things difficult for the Lapps driving their big herds over the borders between Finland and Norway, for example, and in 1852 the border was closed to them. Much trouble had been caused by the big invasion of Finnish reindeer, into the areas that the Norwegian deer had set aside for their winter feeding. When the delicate winter moss, which is pale and spongelike, is destroyed it takes from thirty to fifty years to become suitable grazing again, so the discontent between the groups can be easily understood.

For many years discussions were held, and in 1933 Finnmark was divided into four great districts. It is now laid down when reindeer moss can be taken from a certain district, and when it must be left alone.

In this big region are some twenty-four summer grazing-areas, with ten autumn, winter, and spring ranges.

The reindeer moss is not a rich food, and in a bad winter when the snow is particularly deep and the food difficult to find, life is hard for the deer, who become very thin before the onset of spring. It is then that the long trek to the summer grazing-grounds begins.

From every herd emerges a leader, bolder and stronger than the others, who the entire herd will follow through deep snow, over ice-filled rivers, over the snow-covered fjells or mountains, and through valleys, until the end of the long trail is reached in the spring. They suddenly feel on a certain day, after a period of restless movements, that now is the time to start, and the Lapps have grown so used to this that they prepare for it, and are ready to follow in the wake of the herd, with some of the men keeping watch over them as they move.

The great Finnmark Vidda, a huge desert of snow during the winter, is ideal during these cold and dark months for the big herds, which are now domesticated, to roam freely. Their large hoofs are well adapted for digging into the snow to uncover the soft moss, but if the ground becomes frozen they have great difficulty, and in a bad year food becomes a constant problem, and there is much movement. The Lapp herders must be prepared to travel with the deer, helping them to dig for moss, or even stripping trees for the lichen that can form an emergency diet. Reindeer can stand any amount of cold, and to me it seems remarkable that such a large animal can exist for several months on the moss under the snow. They get very thin during these winter months, then quite suddenly they become restless and feel the spring need for migration to either the coast or the mountains.

A remarkable account of earlier Lapp life, that has now been read throughout much of the world, was given by Professor Johannes Schefferus, the German scholar. His great work, *Lapponia*, published in Latin in 1673, was soon to be translated into English, French, German, Dutch, and more recently into Swedish. He found that many of the old and seemingly fantastic accounts had a good basis in fact, and the 'running on long curved pieces of wood', for instance, was, of course, the Lapps method of moving over the snow on skis for many months of the year. Prehistoric skis have been found in districts in the north and have always been thought to be connected with the Lapps. By using various tests the age of at least one ski has been estimated at about 2,870 years.

The old skis were much wider and more clumsy that the slim modern type, but the principle was the same, and it was from the start a very sensible and also fast method of moving over snow. It is certain that this form of travel forced on the hunters through sheer necessity would never have been thought of by them as a sporting pastime. Every item of their culture, from the thread made from the sinews taken from the legs of the reindeer to the thick winter cloaks made from the deer fur, was designed to keep them alive in a hard climate where the only medical help they ever received came from their *noaides*, or sorcerers, whose magic drums were expected to help them through almost every crisis.

The isolation of the Lapps was rudely broken during the Second World War, for then the whole of Norway was occupied by the Germans. Even the smallest and meanest hut was burned, and the Lapps had to become masters at hiding their herds of reindeer to save them from destruction. Many Lapps were of great assistance to the Norwegian and Allied forces in the latter stages of the war because of their knowledge of the terrain, and the Germans, when they retreated, left nothing behind for either Norwegian fisherman or Lapp in the way of dwelling.

The Lapps had little to lose from such burnings, but the Norwegians, when they returned to the north to rebuild their fishing-villages, had to somehow reconstruct every home and village. It is why today the small groups of wooden houses in the far north always appear so neat and new and well painted. They all have a story to tell. Conditions now have changed for the better, but the old hard life for both fisherman and nomadic herder continues year by year, controlled by the changing seasons.

CHAPTER 2

The Way to the North

THE telephone rang when I was packing. It was my journalist friend.

'Are you really going? All right, I'll be round in about an hour for a picture and a story.'

He appeared, to take a photo, and examined all my equipment with interest.

'How long are you going to be away?'

'About eight months.'

'Eight months! You're mad, but then I always did think your trips were either a long holiday or a mass of hard work. 'I hope you know what boat you're taking,' he said. 'I don't want to write a report and then find you back here again.'

'You had better come to the station,' I replied, glad of his help, for I had collected too many pieces of baggage around me for my own comfort. It is all very well with a jeep and a few others, but when one sets out alone, then it is a different story and every extra item of equipment becomes an added burden that must be taken from place to place and not lost.

I was feeling a bit uneasy. What did I really know of the hard life of these people. It was one thing to sit and read about them, but quite another to try to emulate their life when one was used to a modern life. I could only gather comfort from the fact that I had seen other primitive peoples, and Berit, after all, had been to the Royal Palace. A comforting thought!

I asked myself many times what sort of clothes I ought to take. I had to restrict myself to what I could somehow carry, for I knew that I should receive little help on the migration trek, and everything I had must go on to a sledge. In any case I was taking no foodstuffs, and would have to rely on eating what food they had.

I decided to wear riding-breeches, which I have always found very suitable for expeditions; long wool socks, leather boots, several pull-overs, my tweed jacket, and a shooting jacket.

'You're going to be a bit cold with that lot,' commented my friend.

'The London people said the Lapps will provide me with some of their clothing,' was my optimistic reply to this. We were not to know that no one had told the Lapps this, and that when I finally met them they had nothing for me.

I set out for the train. It was the 1st of April. I hoped that was not a bad sign. The transfer of all my baggage to the North Sea boat was easier than I thought, and the crossing itself was calm and pleasant.

Dawn and early excitement. The air smelt colder and fresher as the long approach to Bergen was made. Everyone was up and eager to see as much as possible.

It was the 3rd of April. Too late to go back now, in any case. The weather was fairly cold, but I was kept warm watching the transfer of my luggage to the old *Vesteralen*, one of the fleet of strong vessels that make the long voyage up the whole length of the Norwegian coast to the North Cape and back, summer and winter.

The boat smelled strongly of fish, but had a homely feeling of age and much use, and the companions I was to have were mainly a group of school-teachers. It would be part of their education, this twelve-day trip to the North Cape and back, and very quickly I had gathered around me a small group of four of the female teachers, all eager to gather all the scraps of information and knowledge of the north that I had read about. The route, in any case, was not unknown to me, and I recalled grimly how I had sailed along it in war days when there was little to smile about.

Now, however, it was a vastly different experience, and one could settle and relax and just enjoy the chatter of the girls. They followed me out on the deck as I filmed from day to day, for the coastline varied every hour in its snowy beauty. Constantly the mountains and hills

1. Aslak Sara surrounded by the main essentials of his life: reindeer, dog, birch tree, the *pulka* or sledge, and lasso.

2. A halt on the April trail to adjust the load.

3. (*Overleaf*) The herders and their reindeer assemble for the spring migration.

4. Berit Sara beside her sledge: her reindeer is a fine beast with near -white fur.

5. Young Nils catching red char through a hole in the ice, using a simple line and hook. He can watch the fish swimming in the clear water.

changed their shapes and heights and formations, and small fishing-villages would appear at the base of the slopes. They rose, it seemed, from the very edge of the water, looking like fresh-painted dolls' houses. Every tiny patch of ground was being cultivated, and one was reminded of a patchwork quilt that seemed to run like a thin band all along the coastline.

The water here can be very choppy, especially in early April, but the ship had the protection of the coastline. This is so broken, jagged and rugged that careful navigation is necessary; however, one had the pleasant feeling of being in a tough safe craft which at any rate is not likely to be mined or torpedoed at any moment. How quickly the years had gone, I mused, as the peaceful landscape swept by, and the many varieties of sea-birds passed in close formations across the surface of the grey water.

The *Vesterålen*, like the others of her line, carried everything that was needed by the villages and small towns along the route. Mail, equipment, machinery, foodstuffs, passengers. These boats are the 'maids-of-all-work' of the coast. It was fascinating to watch the unloading and loading each time we halted for an hour or two at a small pier. Sometimes it was the middle of the night when we arrived, and the long wail of the siren brought a group of villagers rushing to the spot. Electric lights made the scene as bright as a dull day, so there was no problem with the work of loading.

I was standing deep in thought one night when one of the officers reminded me that it was more than seventy years ago that the Englishman Richard With had sailed from Trondheim on the bridge of the first of the regular coastal vessels . . . the original *Vesterålen*. He had worked hard to make this dream of a regular service to the north a reality. I wondered if he had realized just how important the line would become as a summer and winter link between village and town along this coastline that is some 1,000 miles in length.

Herring gulls followed us night and day, hovering close over our heads, and uttering their rather mournful calls as they swung and glided with almost motionless wings on the air currents.

The snow had already left the sides of these mountain ranges which came close to the water in the south. The Gulf Stream, which gives a warming influence here, plays a valuable part in keeping these waters open for fishing all the winter.

We pulled into Trondheim . . . a truly handsome city, proud of its ancient reputation and culture. Around the boat swam large groups of the very attractive male eiders in their striking black and white plumage. It is normally quite impossible to make such close study of these shy birds, but they have learned that the ships mean food, and they gather at once. The females were dull indeed, but they would need their brown plumage to camouflage them when sitting on the large clutches of eggs they would soon be laying further north on suitable and well-liked islands.

The coastal steamer was pulled from the harbour by a small tug that strained and shook at the task. Eventually our engines started up again, and we were once more under way and heading steadily northwards. In these regions the weather changes almost from hour to hour. A bright sun would be glittering on the snow-topped mountains, making us murmur with admiration at the beauty of the light and shade and strength of the ancient and ageless rock, and the next hour a howling wind, with low clouds, would make us glad indeed of the warmth of the lounge. Passengers came and went; there was constant activity, for the ships are used like a bus service, although one must say it takes time to visit another village in this way, and the fishermen mostly use their fishing-boats, of course.

Monday, the 5th of April, was grey with heavy fog shrouding the tops of the snow-covered mountains as we moved through the quiet water. There is something deeply impressive about the quietness. We had reached the line of the Arctic Circle.

There is nothing to indicate this fact other than the statement from one of the ship's officers, but we all felt it was something to celebrate. And indeed we were given a certificate stating that we had come that far! The air, however, did feel much colder, and after several hours on the open deck watching the ever-changing white-capped scenery my face felt very raw and red.

We had to take on board fresh milk, and as we nosed into the tiny fishing-village of Örnes, we were surrounded by hundreds of screaming herring gulls and kittiwakes.

There is much activity around these small fishing-villages and for us it meant that we could load up many churns of milk from one of the coastal farms that cling to the slopes at the foot of every mountain, appearing puny as the giants loom over them.

A little further north and the vessel had to leave the closeness of the coastal rocks and cross over some rather rough water towards the Lofoten Islands.

In the evening, with a grey gloom covering us and making visibility very poor, we reached the shelter of the Lofoten Wall, and the swell that had shaken us like a terrier shakes a rat lessened, for which we were thankful.

The Lofoten Islands are famous for their mighty fleets of fishing-vessels that gather in these waters very early in the year. It is an area of rough seas and tough men, whose work to provide us with fish can be extremely arduous in the freezing cold of a January day and night.

The ship moved even further northwards, passing through fjords whose beauty became more and more intoxicating. So narrow were some of them that one felt it almost possible to reach out and touch the snow on their steep sloping sides.

A fierce snowstorm was blowing as we crept slowly into Tromsø. Here was a name that has been known for many years as the port from which Arctic explorations have set forth.

A constant stream of vessels make their way to this busy place, which now has the reputation of having the longest concrete-span bridge in Europe joining the town to the mainland.

Roald Amundsen, the celebrated Norwegian explorer, is remembered for ever by the town, for an impressive statue of his stern-faced figure stands gazing out over the harbour, from which he himself had set out. The town is proud of him, and as we left the harbour in another blinding flurry of snow I watched until the grey figure was lost to sight in just such conditions that he knew so well.

The *Vesterålen* pitched and strained in very rough weather through the night. A strong wind whistled through the riggings, whilst the grey, cold seas slapped and shot sheets of spray over the decks. At that moment I felt a sense of admiration for those early Norsemen in their longships who had braved these waters, so little then known to them.

In the early hours of a bitterly cold and still black morning we reached Hammerfest, where I was to leave the ship.

Standing on deck, surrounded by all my equipment, I felt very cold and lonely. This was the end of the journey as far as I was concerned with the companions I had made on the voyage, and now several of them had remained up to wish me good luck. I was met by a young man, who had been contacted on my behalf by the Norwegian authorities, and immediately he was questioned by the others as to whether I should have enought to eat, and many other personal questions. He must have found this very amusing, but politely answered everything, and then conducted me to a pleasant guest-house, where I was received with considerable hospitality. Thankfully I crept into a warm bed for a few hours, but was soon wakened, for the Mayor, Anton Eide, was already waiting to receive me and give me a tour of the town, of which they are now all so proud.

Hammerfest was completely and utterly destroyed by the Germans when they retreated from Norway during the Second World War. Not a house of the old wooden-housed town was left. As a grim relic they had left the small cemetery church standing. Photographs taken shortly after the Norwegians returned show the utter desolation around this small church.

There is certainly an air of newness about the town, and this is understandable when one thinks that every house, store, and factory has had to be completely rebuilt.

Deep snow lay everywhere. It was cold and grey, but my tour kept all such thoughts distant for the time being. The fine Town Hall with its many paintings and trophies from the Norwegian life of the past, was proudly shown to me, and in his personal study Mr Eide showed me a painting of my own—of lapwings flying over an English field in winter—that I had sent him some time before. The friendship between Norway and England was clearly visible in Hammerfest, and I was to find the same in every small fishing-village home that welcomed me during my long stay. Photographs of Winston Churchill were more in evidence in the north than I had ever seen in England, and I had to answer a stream of inquiries about the Royal Family.

I was shown a giant mural-type painting of Hammerfest in 1780, found after many adventures in an attic in Oslo. This showed clearly the old wooden houses, the old church and Lapps entering with their sledges.

I had to see the modern schools and the famous factory where so many of the fillets of frozen fish that we buy from our large self-service stores are prepared, and here I lingered for a long time. Dressed in a white overall, I watched with fascination the skill and speed of the girls as they worked with the fish.

And the new church . . . so original, and yet so beautifully conceived, that Hammerfest indeed can be justly proud of its architect.

I remained as a guest of the town for some three days. The smell of fish was everywhere, as was the sound of the gulls as they fought for scraps from the boats.

Hanging on long wires, as they had done all along the coastline, codfish, in rows, were drying in the sun and the wind. For several months of the year these cod hang, drying to a wooden hardness. When they are judged ready, they are packed tightly together in a press, and exported to Africa and Italy. There they can be either used again as fish after being soaked in water or ground into spice powders. Nothing, it seems, is wasted: even the heads are dried in the similar manner and then ground into fish meal for cattle food.

Out of the still waters around the harbour the eider duck still swam in groups. The male eider has one of the most distinctive calls of the north that I know. It carries a long way . . . 'Coo-roo-uh, coo-roo-uh'. Heard at dawn it somehow quickens the pulse. The soberly clad females answer with low-throaty calls of 'Kor-r-r-r—'.

Among the eider floated several pairs of another remarkably attractive bird of the north, the long-tailed duck. The males were still clad in their winter feathering of boldly patterned dark brown and white, and their long pointed tails were clearly visible. Their calls were probably the most musically charming of any of the birds I saw . . . 'Ahh-ahh-alueta'. This is as near as I could write it down, but once heard it is haunting, and a sound that is never really forgotten. They, too, would soon be seeking nesting-places along the north islands.

Hammerfest was far too civilized for me to remain, of course, but it had been most gracious of the town to make me their guest for some three days. Another journalist came to visit me for an article in the local newspaper, and offered to drive me the long and difficult way to the little outpost of Masi, deep in the heart of the big Vidda or plain. This was a tremendous help, for it was a long trip, and the road was still slippery and ice covered in many places.

It was late afternoon when we reached the small group of simple wood houses that formed Masi. This was the last small trading-outpost at the edge of the great plain. A tiny wooden chapel hut stood at the edge of the group, and a few hut-like houses straggled along the banks of the great wide, deeply frozen Alta river, which is so important and busy all summer.

A little knot of Lapps gathered as I was unloaded from the jeep. I was very relieved to find they were expecting me. My journalist companion took charge of the proceedings and soon had all my equipment unloaded into a tiny hut, opposite the store, which had been set aside for me. There I could be comfortable, for a wood-burning round iron stove was in one corner, and this had been laid ready.

The whole place reminded me of an early Western film with the store as the centre for all activities. Here was the post office and the meeting-place for the Lapps when they arrived by sledges from their winter homes far out on the Vidda. When the reindeer had been tethered the Lapps could warm themselves for several hours, squatting round the wall of the large room which served as a kitchen and living-room, and which was always kept warm from a big iron stove.

This was the first time I had had the opportunity of tasting Lapp cooking, and of eating reindeer meat. There had obviously been much speculating about my appearing at this outpost, and I felt that I was on trial as I sat down with the two Lapps who had charge of the store.

They were a rather typical, elderly couple, who had long ago given up nomadic wandering for a more settled existence. 'Aunt Marit' was the picture of plump good health and good cheer. She had a round, reddish face and sparkling eyes that were always ready to smile, and with sleeves rolled right up and her grey hair pulled back, she was obviously a hard worker. Her meal was simple but filling . . . boiled potatoes in their jackets, placed on the table in the saucepan in which they were cooked and a big pot of reindeer meat that was also boiled. We helped ourselves from these pots, but as there had been no flavouring whatever put into the cooking, I found it rather tasteless. There was plenty of home-baked rough rye bread, margarine, milk to drink, and a big portion of genuine Lapp blood pudding to follow as a dessert. I had never before seen blood pudding in this form, and when the dark red mass was placed on my plate I tried to eat it with a will, for the others found it delicious when thickly covered with sugar.

Blood pudding is a dish that takes time to appreciate! It is rich in value as a food, but difficult to stomach at first, and after a few spoonfuls I had to decline more. The young man who was the driver of the snow-mobile that carried mail and passengers over the wasteland of snow in winter, looked at me with great amusement as I tried to eat, and the old man, Turi, Marit's husband, creased up his broad flat face into a thousand wrinkles as he laughed at the weak stomach of the Englishman. He was a very short man, with grey hair, and was a perfect partner for Marit. They knew everything about everyone, it seemed, and they certainly had the opportunity of listening to all the gossip, and of seeing the rare mail that arrived for the Lapps whose winter quarters were scattered over the wide plain beyond.

There is nothing wasted with a Lapp meal, and after the meat and potatoes had been eaten the couple got down on the floor with their large knives and began to hack the large bones to pieces. Small pieces of bone flew about the room, but the reason for all this effort was soon apparent; they were after the marrow. Again I found this hard to refuse and also hard to eat, but one has to be polite and I knew that this was also an excellent part of the deer if one is thinking in terms of food value. For a people who have had to use whatever Nature provided for centuries, it was impossible for this couple to break away from their traditional ways of eating now they had settled down, and could have anything from their supplies in the store.

This first evening meal was finished with bread and cheese, and in honour of my arrival they even made tea to drink. Marit was most anxious that I show her exactly how an Englishman makes a pot of tea. I have always found this amusing on my travels; it seems that there has grown up some mystic ritual in the minds of non-tea-drinkers about the way that tea should be made, and they are always most willing to watch so that in future they can say they know exactly how to 'make tea'. As the tea-bag is so much in use all over Scandinavia, with its poor and comparatively tasteless contents, one drinks a good cup of tea with real relish.

I showed Marit, who had a teapot which she had not used for years, how we warmed the pot first, then placed the tea in it, and after that the really boiling water. We let the pot stand for a few moments, then poured out. Her eyes sparkled with good humour and pleasure as she saw how I enjoyed my drink, and both the Lapps and the young man eating with us also said how good it was. After all, it was a change for them also, for they are used day after day to the strongest of black coffee, into which they put no milk as a rule. For sweetening, it is usual for a cube of sugar to be held between the teeth, through which the coffee is drawn.

That first night I retired to my own small hut, which was extremely warm from the wood fire, feeling drowsy and well fed, and a long way from Cambridge. I had at any rate reached the first outpost, and I must confess that my heart beat faster at the thought of what awaited me when my journey by reindeer and sledge began. How many days I had to wait at Masi was impossible to know, for Lapps come and go as they please without consulting a watch, and I knew that Berit would arrive— as the couple at the store had heard—very soon now for the family supplies for the spring migration trek . . . and also for me.

6. The ice on the river is beginning to melt, and water for the coffee pot comes from the fresh streams.

7. A family party on the fishing-boat crossing to Seiland. The photograph shows Ole Gaino, Karin and two of their boys.

8. Shying away from the ramp leading to the 'pram', the reindeer circle round the herders.

CHAPTER 3

Arrival at the Winter Home

MASI lies on one bank of the big Alta river, which flows through the vast Vidda, or plain, and onwards through the Lapp town of Kautokeino, some distance further to the south. There is a fine Internat, or Lapp boarding-school, at this town, where the Lapp youngsters can obtain a sound education at the expense of the Norwegian Government. It is here that a school of arts and crafts especially for the Lapps was established for the purpose of reviving the old crafts of bone-carving, weaving, basket-making, the making of wooden bowls and many other objects that they had needed for their life for generations past. With the advance of civilization there is always the great risk that the crafts of a people may become lost, and it would indeed be tragic if the Lapp's beautiful and delicate patterned carving and design work on bone were to be discarded for ever. A carved bone sheath for a Lapp knife is something to be really admired for the patience and the skill that goes into its creation.

The next day, when I set out to explore my immediate surroundings, I was amazed at the modern school that had been built in this wilderness setting. It stood a little apart from the small group of old wooden houses that formed Masi, and the pupils spent several months here every year as boarders. The rooms were bright and attractive, and I found the little Lapps charming and took film of the youngest of them learning Norwegian. They were all dressed in their traditional costumes of blue, with many rows of highly coloured red-yellow-green-blue braids, and one small girl with blonde hair and blue eyes looked ready to grow up for a film career. She certainly acted that way for me, and seemed delighted to sit at her studies when I filmed the class. The boys were much more shy, pushing fingers through uncombed hair and looking down at the desks, but the small girls were so thrilled that several of them followed me back to my hut and kept me constant company in the hope of having their photo taken. The sun was now so warm that it was very pleasant to sit on the old wooden steps and try to talk a few words to them.

The language was a little problem, I must confess. I had spent some time learning Swedish, after a meeting with a couple of students in the British Museum in London when I was sixteen. Since that age my interest in Scandinavia had always been very keen, and a slight knowledge of the language was better than nothing, and it was to serve me well. The Lapp children found me difficult to understand and laughed greatly at my speech. They were beginning to master Norwegian, having large books with the alphabet and simple sentences, which were repeated time after time by a most attractive young Norwegian teacher who had come from the south. It is not so easy to draw teachers into the wilderness, but there are many compensations . . . the pay is better, and the wonderful healthy outdoor life that they can have after school hours makes it worth while in many ways. But the towns are soon missed by the majority of them, and it is not the custom for them to remain for any great length of time.

Norway must be admired for the way she has looked after the education of the Lapps, isolated as they are, in the far north of this immensely long and difficult country. Teachers have been wise enough to know that they should retain their ancient language as well as be able to read Norwegian, and in the big Finnmark region a special adviser on Lapp affairs—who is secretary of the Lapp Council—has been appointed. There is also now, of course, the Lapp Society, which was started in Oslo during the war. This has grown into a widespread organization, which has companion societies in Sweden and Finland, all working for the betterment of Lapp conditions in their respective countries.

The children at the school at Masi looked extremely fit and full of life. They had none of the plastic toys seen in such vast quantities in more civilized surroundings, but they did not need them. They were used to skis from the earliest age possible, and most of their time, when the lessons were finished quite early in the day, was spent on races. This was a fine time of the year for them, for the spring was coming after the long and dark winter, and the sun was immensely bright and strong, even though the night temperature was about minus 20 degrees centigrade.

As I did not know exactly when Berit would arrive, I thought I would at least climb to the top of the hill over which the trail led down to Masi. There was still a great deal of snow, which was hard enough at times to support my weight without skis. As I had previously broken an ankle, I had to move with some care, and this caused me some uneasiness. I hoped that this injury from the past would not prove a burden on my journey with the nomads.

At the top of the hill, the slopes of which were covered with many birch trees that still had a sepia appearance, as it was too early for the leaves to appear, the vast plain began. It stretched out before me and disappeared into the blue shimmer of the atmosphere. There were no big trees in this region, merely stunted, dwarf birch, and if ever a region was made for travelling by sledge it was here.

On an early spring day, with a blue sky above and a white desert stretching into a seemingly endless distance ahead, there is a great quietness about the Vidda, and the voice of the crow or the raven or a Lapp dog barking will carry for miles in the thin air.

There were signs of a trail, made by the runners of sledges that had been down to the valley after supplies, and I walked along this for a way until I saw in the distance what looked like a black object lying on the frozen river, that would flow down to swell the Alta waters in great gushes when the thaw really began. The sun was bright against me, reflecting back from the ice, and I could not see what it was at first, but as I approached I saw it was one of the Lapp boys whom I had seen previously at the school.

He raised himself and gave me a cheery grin, showing good white teeth. I joined him beside a small round hole in the ice, and he proudly showed me a pile of red char fish that he had already pulled up. He had a thin line, at the end of which was a bright spinning bait, and as he lay almost flat he could see down into the crystal clear water and watch the fish beneath. Jerking the line up and down constantly, he pulled up fish after fish until a big pile lay as a splash of bright colour on the ice.

Nils, for that was his name, was typical of the boys of the area. His blouse was very worn and patched, as were his trousers, and on his feet were rubber boots. His face was dirty, and somehow I was reminded vividly of the 'William' stories from back home; he seemed exactly like a Lapp edition of that English classic figure. He acted as if he was genuinely glad to see me, and anxious to show what he could do.

After a while he tired of catching the fish, which would be very valuable to his family, whose income was very precarious during the winter months in this region where work was hard to find; and decided to make a fire and cook coffee.

Wiping his nose with the dirty sleeve of his blouse, he picked up all the fish and stuffed them inside the jacket, where they rested on the wide belt, which is so essential a part of Lapp equipment. The jacket-blouse is a versatile item of clothing, and has almost a feminine appearance with its pleated skirt effect. It is most useful when odd things have to be carried and Nils certainly made use of the space in his.

The ice of the river had began to break, and when I looked along into the sun it seemed as if there were a million tiny points of sparkling light being reflected back from the crystals in the water. It was so clear that every stone could be seen at the bottom, and the small trees growing here and there along the banks were reflected sharply. In the midday warmth, with a sky of the deepest blue overhead, it was a place that was as lost to civilization as only this great empty plain can be. The water quietly gurgled and overhead a pair of hooded crows called harshly.

Nils brought out from a bag a battered and very black old pot, which he filled with river water. Gathering birch twigs, he made a fire on the bank of the river. Smoke rose thick from the green twigs, but he did not seem to mind, and fixed the pot over this almost flameless fire. It was typical of the Lapp attitude to ignore smoke, for they are so accustomed to it from the birch twigs, which have to be taken for their fires, where they can be found, from growing trees.

Several of the fish were now pushed on pointed twigs and we held these over the fire. Margarine came from a reindeer bladder, which I soon found was a very usual container, then Nils produced a length of bread, which he cut into chunks with his knife.

The water in the pot soon boiled. The coffee he made was almost as thick as soup, but when he poured plenty of sugar into it, it became a little more drinkable. I watched him as he worked at a meal for us, and if ever a boy was really filled with the pleasure of living it was Nils.

For him there would be none of the problems that seem to beset the lives of the teenagers of our towns and cities; he would have no problems with narcotics, which are the curse of all Swedish towns. He was a product of an age-old pattern of life, and already I felt a thrill at the thought of spending several months with such people.

He looked at me several times. 'Can you understand me?' I asked him when my Swedish seemed very difficult both for him and myself. 'A little,' was his cheerful reply, and he burst out into such merry laughter that it was catching. We sat in the sun, happy and childlike, and enjoyed ourselves.

Nils finished his coffee, washed out the pot with ice-water and cleaned his knife in the snow. Carefully he repacked his margarine bladder, packed his small rucksack, and after donning his skis sped off down the slope towards the household that would be waiting for his catch.

'Slipping along on two pieces of wood, they were able to outpace the wild animals'; so wrote Paulus Diaconus, the Lombard monk, who ventured with great courage into these wild regions in the year 780.

Conditions for the people have changed greatly since those early days, and the great wild herds of reindeer that roamed here have given way to the domesticated groups, but the Lapps still 'slip along on their two pieces of wood' as they have done for thousands of years.

I returned in my slower fashion to Masi. The snow-mobile—a tank-like vehicle that is a tremendous help in the worst terrain—had returned from the nearest collecting-centre with our post. I travelled with it the following day, but it was a trip that resembled a boat in a bad storm, and I cannot recommend it. We plunged down slopes as though falling into a bottomless sea. Everything was thrown in a heap, and in the interior, with its round port-hole windows along each side, it was almost impossible to remain in one position until we reached a level area of snow. The driver had no regard for paths. He headed straight for the trees that lay in his path, proud of his driving skill and of the power in his hands. The small trees disappeared under our tracks, and we drove on ... a relentless modern machine in an ancient wilderness.

The contrast between the old and the new was brought home to me again with great force when he met a very old Lapp coming from the other direction. He was clothed in a cloak of light brown reindeer fur, with big wool mittens on his hands, and a hat of dark blue with the long jester-like points of the district, decorated with many bands of braids, pulled well down almost over his eyes. He wore deerskin trousers and the skaller, or moccasins of reindeer fur, thickly lined with dried grass, which are so essential a part of the Lapp clothing. They keep the feet very warm and dry all winter and are light to wear.

He was at the head of several sledges all loaded with reindeer moss, which he was taking back to his herd.

Both drivers stopped for a chat, as all Lapps do on every possible occasion. The old man, with a face tanned by the weather to the deep brown of cured skin, had merry and bright eyes. He came over and put his arm round my shoulder, and then patted the snow-mobile. He then drew me over to his reindeer, patted its head and indicated that his method of transport was easily the better. We could not converse, for he knew only the ancient Lappish tongue, but we could understand one another easily enough and I also laughed and nodded my head many times. I had some tobacco with me, for one of the things that Lapps do appreciate is a present of tobacco, and when I gave this to the old man his eyes lit up with a pleasure that was worth many times the price of the gift. He felt around among his clothing for something to give me, found nothing, and then scratched his head. He was embarrassed, I could see, so to save his face I went to one of the sledges and pulled off a piece of wood. I held this in front of his face and then put it into a pocket, after which I shook his hand. Honour was saved, and he left us a happy man.

This was the time of year when the nomads were to come down to Masi from their winter hut home, deep in the frozen plain. They had to collect supplies for their spring migration trek. The next day was bright again. Would my stay at Masi soon end? I felt so, and after some hours I was proved right.

Marit Turi was the first to see the figures approaching over the top of the hill.

'There they are. I thought they would come today,' she told me, and I watched the trail and the growing figures with a fast-beating heart. This was the great moment I had been waiting for.

At last we came face to face . . . Berit and I, and it was difficult to know who was more interested in the other. She was not alone, for with her was a man of some thirty-five years with a puckish, cheerful face, pale blue eyes, high cheekbones, and a friendly disposition. He was Ole

Gaino, one of the herders, who was to prove a good friend to me in days to come.

Berit Sara was a surprise to me because of her thinness. It did not seem possible that she was strong enough to make these long trips. Her face was thin, as were her arms. I could not see her legs, because she wore skin leggings, and both she and Ole were warmly clothed in the thick white 'Besks' or cloaks of reindeer fur which are pulled over the head and form a kind of tent. Around the necks of the cloaks were many rows of coloured braids, which were also round their headwear. Warm mittens were pulled off now that the trip to the store was ended, and the sledges that were for the moment empty were left near by and the reindeer tethered and given a pile of moss to eat.

There were three sledges, one for my own use. I looked at the reindeer drawing this and wondered what it would make of me. It looked back at me with curious eyes and drew away sharply when I approached it.

Berit Sara had one of the most impressive reindeer drawing her sledge that I ever saw. In colour it was almost white, with a magnificent set of antlers that weighed heavily on its head. The broad, splayed hoofs that are excellent for travelling over the snow and also for digging for the moss in winter, pawed impatiently at the ground until it was given a pile of moss to eat. It had an appearance of great strength, even at this time when the whole of the herd were very thin after a hard winter and poor feeding.

In comparison, the other two reindeer, pale brown in colour, looked very poor. Berit was proud of her deer, as well she might be. Both the male and female reindeer have antlers, but the females are much smaller. Their small antlers are of great use at times in the spring, however, when the does want to be alone to calve.

A fine buck deer without its antlers, which are dropped each year, looks a very sorry sight. Two knobs stick out, waiting for new antlers to grow, and the whole fine, noble appearance of the animal is destroyed until the even larger set of antlers grow for another season. They can be very heavy, and the bone is long lasting and used for many items of Lapp equipment.

The three sledges were long and painted black. They had wide runners and high backs. It was quite possible to load a great many items on to them, and one could obviously sit in some comfort on the seat at the back, and cover skins over the legs to keep warm.

I looked over the three with great interest before going into the house to join the others.

Berit did not leave me in suspense for long. That she was a business-woman was obvious, for her first words to me when we sat down were:

'Well, what are you going to pay me!' This was a bit of a shock for a start, and I must have looked a little taken aback, for she named a figure which sounded high to me, and then suddenly said: 'We can talk about it later on when we see what happens. But I'm sure you are a rich English-man.'

Only a man who had plenty of money would be making such a trip for several months, was the reasoning of the Lapps, and this I could understand. They had little money themselves, so they saw a good opportunity to obtain an added income for the family, by having me with them on their migration, and for their stay at the coast during the summer.

I packed all my things, loading them carefully on to the sledge I was to use. There was no way of knowing how far we had to travel, and it did not seem that the Lapps had brought any special clothing for me. I viewed this with some misgiving, for without one of their warm cloaks I imagined it would be a very cold ride. There were several reindeer furs in the sledge, however, on which I could sit.

Berit had an extremely high-pitched voice and laugh. There was a good deal of merriment inside the store, and she was being asked many questions about 'her Englishman'. As she was about thirty and still unmarried, the amusement was obvious. For my part I only hoped she would be a bit less businesslike in our relations and a little more personal. It might make things better all round. We could, luckily, understand each other fairly well. Berit was very quick thinking, and seemed to find little difficulty with my rather poor Swedish.

After a warming last cup of coffee we set out. Berit no longer had on her fur cloak, as the day was warm and windless. Round her shoulders she had a thick shawl, in a Scotch-like tartan pattern of red and blue, held at the front with a round silver brooch, over her long blue Lapp blouse.

The three sledges were now heavy, two being well loaded with sacks of supplies, and the third with my belongings. The reindeer viewed them with no delight, I felt sure, and as the snow was soft underneath their hoofs and the sledge runners, conditions were far from ideal for travelling. It is not often that the Lapps move by day at this time of year, for the reindeer prefer the hard, crisp snow at night for easy travel. It would be very tiring for them, I felt, to pull up the first steep slope to the plain.

However, Berit and Ole were in a hurry to get back, for there was much to do, so there was nothing for it but to move, and help the deer as much as possible.

CHAPTER 4

We Prepare for the Great Trek

REINDEER are driven by a long single line that runs on their left side back to the driver. They are harnessed in a simple manner, between two shafts of birch wood that are attached to the sledge by leather strips.

When they are in good condition they can move at a good speed over the snow, drawing a sledge, but like other animals, they can be obstinate and difficult to handle, especially if they feel that the driver has no real control over them.

This was exactly what I feared would happen when we started off, and it certainly did! I sat on my sledge, feeling very insecure, surrounded by my equipment, as we climbed the path that would lead us up the mountain. My reindeer moved a few hundred yards and then stopped, looking round at me with an expression of irritation. I shouted and the others turned back. Berit tied a long lead from her sledge to the head of my deer, and we moved again. Soon we had to leave the sledges, however, and walk beside the head of each of our deer, helping them in their efforts to pull up the sloping side of the mountain.

It was hot, tiring work, for the reindeer, being in poor condition did not have the strength that they would have by the autumn, when they can be used as pack animals, and return over the tundra loaded with possessions on each side of their backs.

At last we reached the top, and turning, took a last look back at the lovely valley, with its little group of houses like toys in a sea of snow. We could trace the winding route of the Alta river for some distance, and the small forests of silver birch trees were a dark sepia that would soon turn to a pale, delicate green.

'Du är flink' (You are clever), exclaimed Berit as we paused for breath, and as a compliment to me she removed the long line that attached her sledge to mine.

I regarded this move with misgivings, and soon I was proved right. My reindeer again refused to obey whatever instructions I gave. It ignored completely all my signals on the line, and I fell back on either cursing at it in English, which it obviously did not understand, or singing, which I hoped would frighten it into quicker movement.

Alas, just when it did decide to move one of the strips of leather holding the shafts broke, and again I was left stranded. I tried to climb along to the offending spot, but immediately sank up to my waist in the soft snow.

In the distance ahead, and growing rapidly smaller, were the sledges of Berit and Ole.

Frantically I shouted. They heard the call, and turned once more, and Ole came back over the trail with his sled to help repair the damage. The only thing we had to use was a strap from one of my camera cases, which proved a good substitute, and soon we had the shaft mended.

Ole set off again, moving as slowly as he could, and every few moments he turned and shouted at my deer, encouraging it to move. Eventually even a Lapp loses something of his humour, however, and another long line was attached between his sled and mine.

We eventually caught up with Berit, who was sitting quietly in the snow, enjoying the sun and rolling a cigarette. All the Lapps carry packets of papers and a quantity of tobacco, from which they make their own cigarettes. Ole sat down beside her whilst I had, at last, a chance to film for a few moments.

We remained at this spot for several minutes, and soon a caravan of sledges came from the opposite direction. Immediately there was a general conversation. These sleds were also filled with reindeer moss, which can only be taken from certain areas at specified times.

Again we moved on, and as I sat on the sledge my feet began to lose all feeling. The air was biting to the face, and I was sure my clothing was going to be inadequate. I had been promised in London that the Lapps would provide me with suitable clothes for travelling, but obviously they had not been informed of this.

I had no idea of how far we had to go, and as the sun began to disappear over the distant hills, and the cold became worse, my spirits sank lower and lower. My hands and feet were freezing, and frost was on my small beard.

Just when I was becoming really worried about frostbite the sound of harsh barking from some of the Lapp dogs at the small settlement of Gargosletten reached us, and soon several of them came running over the snow towards us, followed by two boys on their skis.

Thankfully I saw the three small wooden huts, with smoke rising from their chimneys. The Lapps put on speed and even my deer moved at its fastest pace.

We were greeted by the barking of all the dogs, who sprang around us with yelps of pleasure. From each of the huts children and adults appeared, and I was almost lifted from my sledge and carried into the warmth. Berit and Ole followed me in, and the hot air made my face feel as if it were on fire.

Aslak Sara, one of the Lapp herders, who was also unmarried, sat me on a low stool in the centre of the room, which appeared bare of any furniture, whilst all the Lapps sat around the walls. A hot stone was placed under my feet, and my hands rubbed hard between his.

Feeling began to flow through my body again, but I felt thoroughly embarrassed sitting in the centre of this group as the object of all their curiosity.

Aslak looked with disgust at my leather ski boots, which had been good friends to me on many a lonely walk.

'They are useless,' he indicated, and went to a corner to fetch a pair of the footwear that the Lapps have found to be perfectly suited to their winter needs. These are the 'skaller', made from the head skin of the deer and also skin from the legs, and cut to an age-old pattern. The shapes are sewn together with strong thread made from the sinew taken from the leg. These sinews are pulled between the teeth to shred them into thinner lengths. One length joins another by being skilfully rolled between the hands, until eventually a very strong waterproof thread is made, which the Lapps have used for generations. They have no use for the kind they could so easily have bought in the store.

No socks are worn, but their bare feet are plunged into the skaller, which is padded out with a mass of the dry and very soft senna grass, which is cut and dried into twists during their summer stay at the coast.

This forms a type of hay-box, in which the foot is perfectly warm and dry, and no Lapp would ever start on a journey without some fresh senna grass in his small rucksack to replace the grass that becomes damp with perspiration. Long lengths of webbing are then wound around the top of the skaller and over the skin trousers, and in this way they have a most practical and very lightweight foot and leg covering that cannot be bettered for winter wear. They are useless in the wet, however, but then the Lapps turn to another type of shoe.

I was handed a pair of skaller, for which I was grateful, and also given the place of honour to sleep . . . a very broken old bed in one corner. My new friends merely curled up on the floor, pulled blankets over their heads, and were asleep in the shortest time.

I was indeed thankful for my own bed, on which was a pile of reindeer skins that made a pleasant mattress. These skins are never properly cured as we understand the word, and are always shedding their hairs over everything. This never causes any bother, however, for as Aslak explained . . . 'the hairs soon blow off the clothes in the wind'.

I had arrived at the winter home right in the middle of the preparations for the long spring migration, and no one really had any time to spare to instruct me in anything. On the only rough table that was in the Sara house was margarine, some bread and some cheese. 'Just eat,' explained Berit, and I made the best of this for breakfast, after which I began to feel something of the excitement that gripped the three families that formed this group. To them it was a wonderful feeling of freedom to be again on the move after the long winter months in their isolated position in the heart of this great Vidda. They were all as cheerful as the children and the dogs.

I was amazed at the number of children, but soon I got used to the fact that there were about ten to each family. The sex-life of the Lapps has never really been studied, but after a stay with them I soon found that they were very highly sexed, and made good use of their wide double sleeping-bags of reindeer skin!

The children were placed firmly on small skis almost as soon as they could walk, and soon grew to be as independent as humanly possible. They had no bought toys, much to my relief. Rather they played games that would fit them for their own way of life. One of the boys would run around carrying the antlers of a reindeer in front of his face, whilst his companions would attempt to lasso him. Soon he would find that his skill with the lasso would be needed in a serious manner.

The small girls also were all active and helping in a calm, grown-up manner that impressed me greatly.

The children are given reindeer of their own at an early age, and have their own markings, which are recorded, after much discussion, in a large register for this purpose. The markings consist of a set of cuts from both ears, and there are now a very large variety of these, as no two must be identical. When a young woman marries she takes her reindeer and mixes them with those of her husband, forming a herd that they hope will be enough to support them. It takes some 600 animals to provide a liivng for a small family, so the number of reindeer that a young man or woman has is all-important . . . wealth is recognized in this way, but the Lapps are very secretive when it comes to discussing how many deer they have. To them it is as if they were being asked how much money they had in the bank. It is a private matter, and they never give any exact number, but just make a general sign.

The day was warm, all spirits were high, and the work of packing the sledges proceeded at a fast rate. Tomorrow evening, if all was well, we should be starting off on the long trail to the coast.

During a break in the packing, when Aslak was rolling his cigarettes, I asked him about the wooden huts, which appeared to be new.

'Yes,' he replied, 'I was able to obtain a grant from the Government, using my reindeer as security, so that I could build these winter homes. The wood was brought out by tractor and we built them during the summer when we had the opportunity. But this place is so alive with mosquitoes during the summer that it was very unpleasant, and I was glad when the job was done.'

Just opposite these huts, which were at least clean and warm, even if they were almost devoid of furniture, was another long turf-roofed hut that Aslak told me had formerly housed more than twenty members of three families. It was worse than anything I had seen designed to house animals, and I could well imagine the miserable life that they must have had in such conditions during the winter. Much better indeed are the winter tents, even if these are rarely used today, as the Lapps go more and more over to wooden huts if they can manage to build them with a loan.

The men were all busily repairing the runners of the sleds, and the women packing everything they owned into sacks. They would never leave an item of any value in the huts when they moved, as they assumed they would only be stolen by anyone passing. Berit explained to me that it was for this reason that they had no furniture, but I could well believe that long centuries of a way of life without chairs and tables and other normal home furniture had made them quite unnecessary. They sat on the floor when they ate, and slept on the floor when they were tired . . . it was as simple as that. The greatest puzzle was their washing habits, for although I never found them at all unpleasant, I again never saw them washing. It was one of the mysteries to which I never really did find any satisfactory answer.

Sacks of flour and packets of sugar, packs of dried reindeer meat, and whatever other simple foodstuffs they had, were packed on one sledge, with the kitchen implements, and the whole then covered with thick layers of skins. Ropes secured the packs firmly, for it was essential that the loads would not spill if the sledges became overturned in any bad spots we might encounter on the trek.

There were three families of relatives at the Gargosletten winter home, and the three huts of a simple rectangular design, with their wood-burning stoves, had been placed on the edge of a still-frozen lake. It was an ideal spot for the winter, for the large reindeer herds had freedom of movement to seek out the moss, which had been hard to dig up that winter.

The men did not converse much as they worked, being more concerned with seeing that the sledge runners were in order and that all the items of straps and harnessing of the reindeer were in good condition.

'We certainly don't want to have any further trouble like you had with your sledge,' commented Aslak so that Ole Gaino could hear. They had talked about the way the leather had broken on my sledge, and Ole felt somewhat ashamed at this. I had removed my camera-case strap, for Aslak had fastened a new strap of reindeer leather. The whole of the harnessing was primitive, but effective, and over the backs of the deer went wide bands of highly decorated material, which were fastened under the stomach. From these, shafts of birch—simple poles— were hung. They were attached to the sledges in the most easy manner possible, merely having holes bored through them and strips of leather tied through these to the sledge. Shaped harnesses of light wood were also placed over the necks of the beasts, who took all these activities

9. The view from the island of Vinna was a magnificent vista of small islands and rocks receding into the distance, lit by bright sun on the still water.

10. The author with his hooded crow looking across the fjord: the hut was his summer home.

11. Reindeer of the Sara herd being loaded into the flat-bottomed 'pram' for transport over to Seiland and the summer grazing grounds.

very well. But there was a burst of fighting between two of the bucks when the Lapps tried to draw the line of sledges into an order for moving, and only after a good deal of pulling and dragging at the heads of the animals could they be separated. The whole of the harnessing had to be recommenced, as the straps had been broken, but Aslak said to me philosophically: 'Better now than when we are started. Then we certainly want no fighting.'

The women were naturally more animated, and the laughter and merriment sounded as though they were preparing for a picnic instead of what to me at any rate was an unknown and long adventure. I tried to share their humour, but always had the nagging fear that I might hold them up. However, they were all so friendly with me that I had little fear that we should not get on.

Berit had spoken no more about money, but I had already paid her an amount so that I would be no burden upon them, for I was dependent upon them for food, having brought nothing out with me. I was determined to live as they did.

The most likeable of the herders, to me at any rate, was Nils Sara, at fifty-five the eldest of the children of old Christine Sara, the head of the big family, who I was not to meet until later at the summer grazing-camp. He and his wife Anna had ten children, the youngest of whom, five-year-old Anna-Maria, was as blonde and charming as only a little Lapp girl can be. She was most interested in me, and wandered round watching me. When I turned she would immediately run behind a pile of skins, and peer shyly round them. Nils was very proud of her, and they were a most devoted couple, and never far from each other.

Anna, his wife, showed the strain of years of child-bearing in the distorted shape of her breasts, which hung down under her blouse so low that when she sat it appeared as if she was again pregnant. Lapp women wear no support for their breasts, and year by year they had dropped further. It was a great pity to see her so, for she was a most friendly woman, and Nils and she worked well together. Her face was sharp, dark and high-cheekboned, and her hair and eyes seemed to be almost black.

Josef, quiet, intelligent, slim and very eager to follow his father at fifteen, was free from school for the summer for the spring migration. His elder sister, Ellen, was also a good-looking girl with dark hair, and I thought she would be much sought after by the young men very shortly. The other children were not at the camp, but we should meet them later.

Aslak and Berit had remained unmarried for longer than most Lapps. She was over thirty, and he a little older. Normally they lived with their mother in one of the huts, but the old lady, at seventy-five, did not feel up to making the long migration each spring and autumn now, and would travel to the coast by other transport along the rough tracks and by boat, a little later.

Ole Gaino, who was thin and nervy, but a most cheerful character, had a wife who was solid and calm, and the obvious leader of his family. They had five children, two of whom were at school, the youngest, a year old, was with relatives, and the other two boys were to travel on the trek. Both were very interested in everything I had, especially the cameras, and I found them unspoiled and attractive small boys, who worked hard to help their mother and father with all the packing. Ole's wife, Karin, was a sister of Berit, so it was essentially a family unit that remained together in this way all winter, only to split up and go to different grazing-grounds with their herds in summer.

Berit and Anna chatted in their very high voices, which jarred on the nerves rather, and it was pleasant to turn to Karin Gaino, with her more appealing and deeper voice. Nils Sara spoke quite good Norwegian, and was no trouble to understand. He was fond of his pipe, which he smoked incessantly, and he tried to show his friendship by offering it to me for a few puffs.

Every item that the families possessed was taken out over the snow to be packed. The huts would be left empty at the mercy of whoever passed, but they had nothing to steal, so the Lapps had little fear.

The cooking-utensils were mostly of wood, the bowls being carved from one wide piece. Over the fire would hang the very large black iron pot, suspended by a long iron rod with big teeth so that the pot could be high or low over the fire. It reminded me much of those I had seen in very old houses with open fireplaces in England.

Berit was most careful with the packing of the best of the family clothing. Fine white furs, new and expensively made blouses and well-tanned leggings, all were packed, to be ready for use if a wedding or a funeral was to be attended. Both of these occasions call for the best of clothing, and also for the wearing of the lovely and beautifully made silver ornaments that are worn at the neck, and which are the most valuable of the Lapp's possessions.

'Where are they all kept?' I asked Berit, as I looked at these items.

From her waist hung a big old key. This was for her personal chest, an item which follows every Lapp when he or she travels, and into which every small thing of value is put. The chest is usually oval in shape, not very large, and often painted with the most colourful designs.

Not all the sledges were of the higher variety with the wide runners. Some were of the *pulka* type, a very fast-moving boat-like sledge that a reindeer can pull at a good speed over the snow when necessary. These fascinated me, for they were exactly like boats for the snow, having a long keel instead of runners, and sides built up like a slim rowing-boat. There was a boat-like stern also and a sharp nose. In this *pulka* it was possible to sit and be very close to the snow. They were easy to cover with skins, and were ideal for travelling long distances on the plain.

The very last of the sledges for each group had no back. It was used for the pulling of the long tent poles, which dragged out behind like a tail to the column. The tents and the cloth had to be carried all the time, ready for quick erection when we stopped for the daily rest.

The lines of sledges were nearly ready as the sun began to sink and the temperature drop. We would be waiting until about eight in the evening, when it would be just right for starting. We should travel all night, and then rest for sleep and food in the early morning, and again travel in the evening.

The last of the items to be loaded before we started and certainly, to the mother, the most valuable, was the three-month-old daughter of Elsa, a most attractive dark-haired young Lapp, who was attached to the group, as her husband had become a herder for the family. He was out now with the big herd, as it had to be watched, being extremely restless and eager to move. It would have been impossible to have delayed our starting for much longer, for the reindeer would have dictated their instinctive terms, and the Lapps had no option but to follow in the wake of the animals moving towards their summer goal.

The small baby was warmly wrapped in a number of brightly coloured blankets and placed in a *komsa*, or old Lapp cradle, which had been in her family for many years. She was given a bottle of milk to suck, and lay without fuss, gazing at the sky with wide, dark eyes.

The *komsa* had been made by her grandfather many years before, and bore some resemblance to a *pulka* in general shape. It had a curved wooden base, over which was tightly stretched a sheet of warm brown reindeer skin. This continued right up to form a hood over the head of the child. Lacings of braid held in all the clothing under a further sheet of skin and fur, and over the whole *komsa* was draped a piece of coloured cloth to keep the cold night air from the face of the small girl.

Strong braids made it possible for the *komsa* to be carried over the shoulder when walking, and when Elsa came from the hut with her load in the evening light she sank almost to her thighs in the snow. The rest laughed at this, but she pulled herself out and made the baby very comfortable on the sledge. She was expected to make the long journey at this early age. Here was another little Lapp who was really born to the ancient trail.

The sun that had so warmed the open Vidda all day now sank behind the distant hills in a glowing red ball, making the snow a vivid pink and at once the temperature began to drop.

It was the evening of the 21st of April. There was no talking now. the glow from the pipes of the three men with the caravan showed blobs of yellow-red. Nils moved to the front. The bell hanging from the neck of his leading reindeer clanked unmusically as the first deer moved forward and pulled at its load. The whole of the columns then began to draw forward and the sound of the clanking bells sounded loud in the silent air. The barking of one or other of the dogs was quickly silenced by a shout from one of the men.

The sledges were now heavily laden, with the small boys well wrapped in furs. Little Anna-Maria had a warm covering of a thick white cloak of fur, over which she wore a bright shawl of scarlet and blue, and over the *skaller* on her feet were bands of red for binding round her leggings. On her head was a red hat, pulled well down over her ears, and embroidered with many braids. She looked warm and comfortable, and most decorative.

I was settled at the rear of one of the larger sledges, also well bedded down on several furs, and wearing a thick cloak, which Nils had been kind enough to lend me.

We had started on the two-hundred-mile trail that the old family had followed for generations, and which they knew intimately; over still frozen rivers, and mountainsides.

It was with mixed feelings that I felt the sledge begin to move under me. But the trek had begun, and there would be no turning back. Above us the sky was now a deep blue, the stars twinkled with great clarity, and I silently prayed with real earnestness that I would not be any bother to these friendly people who asked so little from life and who seemed to know the meaning of being happy.

CHAPTER 5

Drama of the Migration

B Y nature and instinct the reindeer is a herd animal. In the past great numbers gathered together in winter months in the wild state. This gave them more protection against packs of wolves, probably their chief enemy.

Now the vast wild herds have gone, to be replaced by the big domesticated groups, but the pattern of the life cycle is the same, and the nomads have been forced to adapt their life completely to the natural instinctive movements of the deer.

The huge Finnmark Vidda is ideal for the winter months, but in summer it would be death for the animals. The whole plain then becomes impossible because of the great numbers of mosquitoes and gadflies, the terror of the reindeer. At all costs they must escape; either into the heights of the mountains, where the atmosphere is cooler and they can be at peace, or by long treks to the coast, where the vegetation is good and they can also be free from the flies.

The insects lay their eggs in the ears, the fur, and even in the nostrils of the deer, and the larvae of one species even burrows under the skin and into the throat, and also along the back. After this, they grow until they are ready to emerge, when they are usually shaken loose by the deer in its efforts to rid itself of the pest. They then turn into chrysalises and eventually into flies.

The reindeer become very weakened by these flies, lose weight and know no rest. The larvae 'wander' over their backs under the fur, making breathing holes which can greatly destroy the value of the skin.

The soft moss on which they have existed all winter becomes dry and crumbles into dust, so their food supply is lost for several months. Thus it was that centuries before the Lapp hunters first thought of the idea of taming the herds for their own use the deer migrated in their thousands each season of the year; to the traditional mating-grounds and also far calving for the summer; for the rutting in the autumn and then back to the winter ranges.

As we moved I marvelled that this migration has altered so little during the centuries. In the midst of all the changes of the civilized world here was a pattern of life that had remained almost constant.

Now ahead of us moved the big shadowy herd. There was no real darkness. The snow was clearly visible against the velvet of the night, and in the cloudless heaven the millions of points of light seemed nearer than I had ever known. In the clear air even the smallest sound carried over a long distance. The Lapps were silent as they moved, but the sound of the sledge runners was like the swishing of waves on a shore.

The herd ahead trampled the snow with thousands of wide-splayed hoofs, and in their very light-coloured winter coats they seemed in the curious light of the night to move like one huge restless wave. The reindeer is not a noisy animal. The only sound it makes is a hoarse deep grunt, and this, plus the sound of the tinkling bells at their throats, made a soothing symphony that lulled the senses almost to sleep.

I had been given a sledge of my own with a reindeer to draw it that I could see had no respect for me! Turning, I saw the children also huddled in their furs on their sledges. They made no noise. Mostly they slept, for sleep comes very easily to a Lapp, and the gentle motion was like the rocking of a cradle.

The dogs gave an occasional bark, but they were quickly silenced by Aslak or Nils, who I could see at times as they went back and forth along the flanks of the herd on their skis. From my own big reindeer the breath rose in a thin cloud, as it panted to keep its place in the line. The snow was just right under us, very crisp, and the cold night air made the work of the pulling deer easier.

The dogs are as much a part of the Lapp scene as those of a shepherd in his world. They save the herders a great deal of time and effort, for they are intelligent and quick moving, usually with short legs that seem to make good progress even in soft snow. Mostly they are pointed-

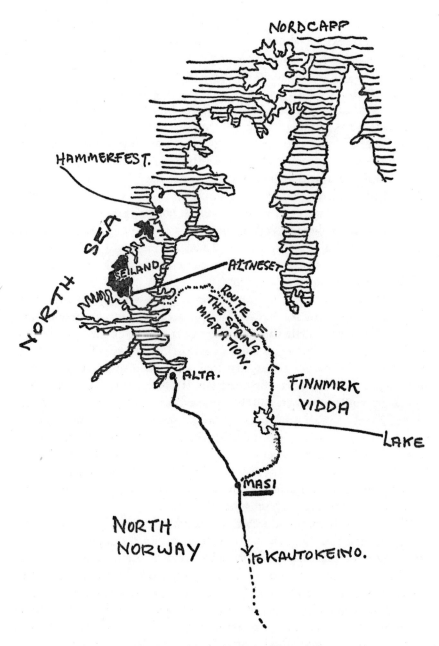

ROUTE OF THE SPRING MIGRATION

eared Pomeranians; quite small, light in weight and a mixture of either very dark brown or almost black, or a blend of white and black, or possibly a pale brown. I had already made friends with one fine dog that I secretly hoped I should be able to take back to England with me in the autumn. It was larger than the others, in general appearance much like the Eskimo sledge dog, with soft long brown fur and a bushy tail. The owner was a young herder who was away for a time with another group, and for some reason had left the dog behind. I had noticed in the few hours that I was helping with the loading for the journey that it had seemed lost and in need of human company. Probably because of this it had attached itself to me, pushing its noble nose into my hands and looking up at me with large and almost human eyes.

Now it ran beside my sledge, and I felt a feeling of growing attachment for this really lovely animal. I had lost my own faithful pet in rather tragic circumstances, and now came the hope of having found, after long searching, a replacement.

As the night began to progress it was as if the whole body started at last to relax and unwind. In the almost intoxicating atmosphere of this still and beautiful northern light, short as it is even at this time of the spring, the human thoughts seem to go back over the whole of life. I found myself thinking of my first love affair, of a quiet English river in June, of the thrill of the first early nests I had found as a boy, of the loss of my father, mother, and then grandmother, all great lovers of the wilds. After a time a great sense of sadness crept over me, so much so that I called to the dog by my side for company. It came near me, and I reached out to pat it and talked softly. It wagged its tail and perhaps felt the same need for friendship as I did. These sentiments may appear strange, but at the time and in the circumstances they were very real and the dog kept at bay my sense of isolation.

Each of the herders had either one or two dogs, and although they made no real fuss of them, there seemed to be an understanding between dog and man that is only to be found when there is a closeness day and night all the year round. The puppy is trained from an early age by its master, and many times I saw a dog curled up by the side of the Lapp as he slept. There seemed little difference between the two. Both knew their work and relied on the other, and it was normal that they almost shared the same food. Often the dogs are fed on a soup of blood and flour which is cooked and given to them morning and evening.

Empty reindeer stomachs are filled with blood at the time of slaughtering, and this can be either dried or frozen for future use. And of course the dogs enjoy all the scraps that remain from the meals.

In the same way that a shepherd has a series of calls that his dog obeys, so has the Lapp herder. The two work well together in rounding up a group of deer, or chasing after a single animal that has strayed from the herd. There is work for them all the year round. In winter they accompany the herder on the long night watches, keeping the herd under control, and in summer they follow him as he makes his rounds, for the deer must always be guarded. A great many accidents can happen, especially in the areas of high mountain rocks and valleys towards which we were heading.

The night slipped away quickly. The going had been quite even and good, but my limbs now felt cramped and in need of stretching. When dawn gradually crept back into the sky my blood ran quick with the thrill and sheer glory of that first early sunrise on this old trail where the rest of the world seemed to cease to exist.

Over the line of distant low hills the sun appeared, bathing the whole of the snow-covered Vidda in a soft yellowish light. It promised to be a fine day again, and it made me realize how cold I really was. The temperature during the night had fallen to about minus twenty degrees centigrade.

Nils gave an order and the caravan came to a halt on the flat white plain. There was no wind, only a great quietness, broken by the sound of hooded crows, black against the snow, that were keeping up with us in the hope of food scraps, and the grunts from the reindeer. The big herd ahead of us stopped also, and one by one the animals sank to the ground, or began to paw under the surface for moss. They would not wander far, but an eye would have to be kept on them all day, and this was also where the dogs were of such great assistance.

The children were quickly up from the sledges, bright and full of energy and eager to help as best they could. They had been sleeping all night whereas everyone else had been busy. The boys were sent to gather twigs of birch for the fire which they were soon chopping up. Meanwhile the adults dragged off the tent poles and cloth and began the task of making camp for the day, for we should remain in this spot until the evening.

The Lapp tent is an excellent example of a simple but effective dwelling that has served in the past for living through the coldest winters and also in the heat of the summer. Even with only a few milli-metres of material between the family and the bitter low temperature of winter, it is enough protection; for the floor is always thickly covered with birch twigs, over which more coverings of furs are laid. These go some way up the sloping wall of the circular tent to keep out the draught, and when the fire is alight in the centre, with the smoke escaping through the big hole left in the top, the warmth of the family seated around the walls makes the interior cosy, if at times extremely smoky.

Nils and Aslak dragged out the supporting framework first and erected it quickly. Four curved poles, joined together in pairs, made the arched rafters. These rafters had a round bar connecting them at the top, and it was from this that the cooking-pots would be hung. Half-way up the sides of the poles there were also two cross-bars parallel to the smoke-pole, which itself was slotted through the arched rafters. Two other poles, with holes at the top, fitted over the end of the smoke-pole to form the doorway, and then around this framework, which was sturdy and had been evolved through much experiment in the distant past, poles of birch of about fifteen feet long were placed. Thus was made a cone-shaped tent, about fifteen feet in diameter.

This took the two men only a few minutes to erect, and I helped them with the poles, to gain experience. The sledge with all the tent material was naturally right against the site of the tent for convenience. The tent cloth, which was in two sections and of a sail-cloth, greenish-grey material, was then pulled around the poles, leaving a large hole in the top, through which they came to a point. It reminded me vividly of the tents I had seen in the old books of the North American Indians, although there were many differences.

The two edges of the material met at the doorway, but the door itself was a separate item, being a further piece of material that hung down and could be pulled up by a string. The boys, who had been gathering armfuls of twigs during this time, strewed them thickly all over the floor, except for the fireplace in the centre, which was surrounded by stones. Over the twigs, piles of our furs were then laid. Thus quickly and without the least fuss a comfortable and pleasant tent had been erected which could house a family. I was later to hear from old Chris-tine Sara, Berit's mother, that several of her children had been born beside the fire in just such a tent, which I thought was far more hygienic than some poorly built hut. These tents can be moved without much trouble at any time, and their design is certainly excellent.

Ole Gaino and his wife Karin were erecting their own tent, while their two sons gathered wood, and soon smoke from the holes in the top of the tents was rising in grey columns in the still air. Birch twigs burn with plenty of smoke, unfortunately, and my eyes got terribly irritated whilst the food was prepared. It became impossible for me after a few minutes, for my eyes were very sensitive after the cold air of the night, and I found it better to sit outside in the warmth of the rising sun and eat my food on my sledge.

It is amazing how quickly a Lapp woman will prepare a warming and filling stew in the big old round iron pot. They are expert at making fires under almost any conditions. Berit always had with her a good many pieces of very thin birch bark, which burn with a fierce flame with the first match, because of the oil they contain. The dwarf birch trees covered the plain in their thousands, and the thin twigs that we broke off for the fire were full of fresh sap and buds that were ready to break out into the attractive fluttering leaves of the summer. It was because of this that they smoked so badly, but even so they gave out a good heat, and when the boys had taken out an axe and chopped a pile of thicker branches, then there was enough heat to make a meal and to boil the coffee water. As for the stew it was a somewhat tasteless dish, however, because they never seemed to season their food at all, and even fine reindeer meat needs seasoning. No salt seemed to go into the boiling of the potatoes either, but as I had none with me, I made the best of it. The food was probably healthier that way, I mused. I shared my hot stew of meat and potatoes with my dog, which lay at my feet and appeared to have completely adopted me. It was a pleasant feeling, but my cheeks began to burn like fire, so when I had eaten the food I coated my face with cream which I had bought for this purpose.

Berit saw me doing this. She came over and sat beside me on the sledge.

'Can Cox sell me some of that?' she asked. She always called me 'Cox' in her thin high voice. None of the Lapps could say 'Hugh' at all, and Nils made the best compromise by calling me 'Brandon', which is a name they could all say easily.

'Have as much as you like,' I replied, with a smile, and she sat happily looking into the small mirror I had and smearing the cream over her cheeks. I was sure she did not need it, but it had a pleasant smell, and it gave her a lot of pleasure. Ellen also came over, as did little Anne-Marie and I could see I had started something that was going to be difficult to stop. Fortunately I had two jars of cream, and one I gave to Berit, telling her to share it with the others if they liked to use it. Soon little Anna-Maria had her face smeared with it, as did Ellen, and Nils came over to me, shook his head, and said with a laugh:

'I hope you haven't got anything else they'll want to use. You will lose it all if you have. I sometimes wonder how it will go with Ellen. She has already got a taste of modern ways. It isn't so easy for a young girl to take to this life now when they see how easy people can have it in modern homes. But I don't think she will leave us. It made me think of it when I saw her with your cream. It was easier for a girl when Anna and I were married, for we did not see much of any modern life. The war made a great difference, you know, Brandon.'

He sat deep in thought for a time. He was older than I, but we had both played what part we could during the war, when the Germans had occupied Norway, and the Lapps had been forced to hide their herds, and indeed take an active part in the fight for liberation.

Nils was a very sympathetic and deep-thinking man. He appeared to like me, which gave me a warm feeling, for I could not have really blamed the group if they had shown me little friendship. I was a foreigner, and they had no idea what I would write about their way of life. It was to them like a stranger coming into any home in England, observing how we live, and then writing about it. One had to win their confidence and respect, and show that there was a genuine interest, from my side, in their life.

Ellen had been grinding coffee beans in an old wooden grinder with a handle on the top. It took her some time, but the result was good coffee, if much too strong for me. Milk came from tins, to which the Lapps added water. Sugar we carried as well as bread and margarine, and it was not long before we had all eaten a filling meal in the early morning. The women all asked me how the night had gone for me, and whether I had been too cold. I told them it had been wonderful, and they smiled at my enthusiasm.

As we sat a pair of ravens flew over us on huge black glossy wings. Their far-reaching calls of 'Unnc-unnc' formed the most fitting background music to this wild place that one could imagine. The sound of the crows, the grunts of the deer, the occasional barking of the dogs . . . one could well understand why the small baby was so little trouble, and that she would grow up to have the strong nerves of the others. I watched her as her mother fed her, showing her breasts to me in the most natural manner. The child sucked happily, and the young mother looked up at me with pleasure in her eyes. It made a fine sight, this mother bending over her small child, close to the snow, yet warmly wrapped. The whole of the camp looked peaceful, with the line of sledges ready to move again at night. The draught deer—those pulling the sledges—had been turned loose, but they would not go far, and could be easily caught again in the evening.

It was time now for us to sleep. For the Lapps this was very easy. They merely lay down on the furs, curled up like the dogs, and pulled a thin blanket right over them to keep out the light, which was rapidly becoming very strong. At midday, when the sun is shining, the light is a burden, I found, for the reflection back from the snow is tiring in the extreme. Sun glasses were very necessary.

It was our intention to sleep, and not to move, during the day. But for me sleep came far more slowly. My own dog was curled close to my head, and its quiet breathing helped me eventually to doze off, despite the light. The smoke had disappeared from the tent now that the fire was dead, but the strong sunlight coming through the hole in the top did not bring sleep as quickly as did the sense of warmth and drowsiness that came from the close sleeping bodies around the walls. They were like contented children.

In the mid-afternoon the dogs and then the families began to stir again. Rising, the Lapps shook themselves like the deer, and the loose hairs from the furs flew from their clothing. I also rose, took some water that had been in a pot all day over the fire space, and washed and shaved. The Lapp herders must have washed at times certainly, but it was difficult to ever find them shaving. And they seemed to need a razor very seldom. But they were all clean in their habits, and the women always managed to look tidy despite the journey. Their big colourful tartan shawls seldom left their shoulders, and, of course, they wore leggings of skin and the fur *skaller* on their feet, so they had little real problem. Hair was mostly combed straight back, and parted in the middle.

Another meal was prepared so that we should start again well fed before the night's trek when the whole camp had to be packed, and the tents dismantled and repacked on the sledges. This went smoothly and without fuss, and I was told that I could get on with writing up my notes each day, and taking my films, as my help was not really wanted. That I could readily believe!

There was one surprisingly modern feature of the trip over which Aslak Sara was very proud. He was the owner—on hire-purchase at any rate—of a brightly painted yellow snow-scooter, which was proving a great benefit to him. He had sold some deer to pay the first instalment and would pay off the rest in about four years. He could now travel at a fine speed over the snow and saved himself many long tiring trips on skis after the deer. Aslak showed in his face that he was the driver, for the engine covered him with soot until he resembled a sweep. The scooter could draw a considerable weight behind it on the migration, but Aslak was usually to be found way ahead of the herd scouting the trail, and we had sufficient deer to pull our loads.

When I laughed about his black face he sat beside me, wiped it as best he could, then said: 'I think down in Oslo they imagine we Lapps have horns on our heads and a long tail.' At that moment, dirty as he was, it would not have surprised me to have seen him with a tail! We both laughed about this, but Aslak would not have changed his snow-scooter, having found what a great help it was. Nowadays these scooters have become a part of the daily life of the north and are growing in popularity year by year. The police patrols of the mountain regions also find them a wonderful aid. Another item that these isolated Lapps had, that also saved them much leg work, was a 'walkie-talkie' set. Nils and Ole could keep contact over a long distance with this, and in summer, with the herds, they found this very useful. So modern aids had begun to come to the Sara family, but otherwise the old way of life was little changed.

The noise of the snow-scooter was greatly disturbing in the vast silence of the plain, and quite suddenly Aslak frightened up a few ptarmigan, which rose almost invisibly from the snow in their white feathering, and flew off with harsh cries. They then showed their black tails but had been quite unseen by us until fear forced them to fly.

As we were settling in the next morning for the day's camp, after another very fine and smooth night's run over the plain and also over the flat surface of a big frozen lake, one of Ole Gaino's sons came over

12. Five-year-old Anna-Maria on the long spring trek, warmly wrapped in thick fur cloak, leggings and moccasins.

13. Aslak Sara surrounded by the herd at the assembly point opposite the island of Seiland waiting to be transported in the 'pram'.

to me with a beautiful plump ptarmigan swinging head down from his arms. Ole had shot the bird, leaving Karin and his other son to erect the tent while he went on a short hunting excursion. Fresh food was always very welcome and we had seen a number of ptarmigan, which belong to a small group of birds that are resident in the Arctic regions. They have soft white feathers reaching down to around the feet to help them over the worst winter spells.

Ole had been most useful in providing us with several of these birds, which make excellent eating. Also young Aslak, another of Ole Gaino's sons, was almost as good at catching red char as the boy Nils had been at Masi; so we managed to have a welcome change of diet even in this white wasteland. Young Aslak was a very serious boy of about eleven and his brother was a year younger. Both were very thrilled with their way of living, and copied every action of their father, who was a good hunter.

I felt that Ole would have no difficulty with his sons, because they also had a calm and capable mother in Karin, who treated her husband rather like a small boy at times, as they all seemed to do. Ole certainly was very much like a schoolboy. He was as thin as I, and smiled at me repeatedly with a wide grin. I believe that if he and I had been left alone together there is no knowing what adventures or troubles we would have got ourselves into. As it was, Karin controlled us all in a pleasant and happy manner, and Ole had to content himself with his short hunting expeditions. He moved very well and quietly on his skis, and as he knew the value of every rock and clump of birch trees for shelter, he was fairly successful with his gun. All the herders carried a rifle, a single shot, quite simple and light. Unfortunately, they often had to shoot a reindeer during summer that had fallen and broken a leg. When on the winter and spring watches over the herds they could at times bring down a bird or even a fox, and the very fine thick fox pelts were certainly worth having.

Berit soon had the several ptarmigan plucked, and that late afternoon our meal contained game bird, eaten under a beautiful early spring pale blue sky, and washed down with a couple of glasses of sherry, from one of three bottles I had brought with me in my luggage for special occasions. Nils, Ole and Aslak drank from their deep brown carved wooden mugs and rolled the liquid around their tongues for a while before swallowing it. I looked at each of their faces for a reaction.

'Very good, Brandon,' said Nils, reaching for the bottle to examine the label with interest. They each smelled the contents, poured out another drink and asked me if I had more bottles.

'What little I have will have to last us for a long while, I am afraid, and I think what we will do is to keep it to celebrate whenever something really important happens,' was my guarded reply. I was secretly wishing I had a big supply, for I found the warming influence of the sherry made the journey much easier.

This remark caused the three Lapps to break into a laugh and begin a very animated conversation in Lappish. Nils explained to me a little later that they were trying to decide what would be 'the important occasions', and each had different ideas. Would I think that it was the landing of the herd on the island of Seiland for the summer after this trek: would it be the first calves very soon to be born; would it be the big autumn round-up and marking; or would it be a possible wedding? It gave them food for much speculation, because of the possibility of having another drink. Brännvin, the clear colourless strong spirit of the north, was expensive and difficult to obtain except when they had money in the autumn. A little drink was welcome indeed, and because of the rare atmosphere, quickly felt in the head.

Some nights later the weather suddenly changed. The wind came screaming over the Vidda, unchecked in its fury, and we were forced to stop our march onwards. The curtain of white thrown up made a dense fog through which we moved with the misty appearance of characters in a dream. It was past midnight, but it was obvious we should soon have to stop in such a storm. With a low sobbing moan the icy air tore across the seemingly endless stretches of snow-covered plain over which we were slowly trying to make our way.

Nils shouted the order to halt and the sledges were drawn into a circle, with the reindeer straining against us as we dragged on their leads. They hated the searing wind and were now difficult to handle. For the first time I was to experience the fury of the north instead of the calm I had begun to accept as normal. The contrast was brutal, and it was hard to even breathe. The Lapps took it all serenely, however, and soon, by some miracle of good management, we had a tent cloth pulled over our heads, and the sledges at our backs. The snow quickly began to pile in drifts against the sledges, making a wind-break, and in our improvised shelter we were soon fairly warm and ready to remain until the storm blew past, which Nils thought might not be for several hours.

There was nothing for it but to curl up and try to sleep. This was the Lapp philosophy and I had to accept it also. Some of the dogs were at our feet, and the big herd of reindeer ahead of us had sunk down into the snow to ride out the gale. Josef, sitting next to me, unconcerned, pulled out a big bone with plenty of dried meat still on it, and began to cut long strips from this with his knife. We chewed on these and he swallowed his quickly and with relish. I found I had to munch mine until my jaws ached before it seemed ready to swallow, but this dried meat is an essential part of the Lapp diet and is often dropped in thin slivers into cups of coffee.

The night seemed long, but with the dawn the wind passed, whining away into the distance and leaving behind a great silent void. We were glad to creep out from our shelter into the cold light of the rising sun. The sledges were almost invisible under the snow, and had to be dug and dragged out to the surface again. Day had dawned, so it was useless to think of moving now. The tents were pulled out and set up and a camp was prepared. The sun would make conditions very bad during the day with this newly driven snow, and this was one of the many set-backs that had to be accepted. When I asked Aslak how long the journey usually took he replied that it depended entirely on the weather. If they had a good run, then perhaps it was about two weeks, but it could be longer if the spring storms hit them. So far during our week's travel we had been fortunate.

Soon all was quickly activity again, with the boys searching for twigs as usual. There was never any need to give instructions to them; they knew what to do, and were proud to have their own jobs. Even Anna-Maria tried to help her mother by carrying what she could to the tent.

CHAPTER 6

Hazards of the Trail

THE days and nights of the trek, which was perhaps some 150 to
160 miles or more, in length over no visible trail whatever,
continued to pass in a ritual of day rest—or only attempted rest on
my part—and night travel. The light of the day was a constant problem
which I never solved satisfactorily. The Lapps would be sleeping,
breathing deeply and calmly, all round the wall of the tent, with blankets
pulled right over their heads. But when I tried this it felt stifling and I
had to pull mine off to breathe, then the glaring light coming through
the hole in the top of the tent would almost blind me. I was thankful
for the evenings, which brought a softer light, and also for the long
night travel which gave me a better chance of rest. My eyes, which had
always been rather sensitive, were now suffering badly from the thick
smoke and light in the day tent, and from the contrasting freezing air
by night.

Some of the rivers and streams we had to cross with the herd were
already beginning to rush with melting snow water, and we had to
search for shallow crossing-places. Fortunately the men knew exactly
where to look, for they were accustomed to these things and took it all
in the night's run. It was amazing how well Nils, who was really the
leader of the caravan, knew every mile of this seemingly uncharted
wilderness route. Every mountain contour, lake and river was known to
him, and this knowledge was of the greatest value when it was necessary
for us all to cross a river just opening up from the winter's freeze.

Early one morning, after a long crossing over a still-frozen lake, where the going had been fast and smooth, we came to just such a small river where the water had begun to show. It sparkled in the early morning sunlight, but it was a dangerous spot, for we had no sign of just where the banks were, because of the snow drifts on either side. The most important thing was to protect the equipment and sacks of foodstuffs on the sledges from the water, so the best possible place to cross had to be found.

Nils called the sledges to a halt and tested, with his stick, the depth and hardness of the frozen snow that stretched over the river like a bridge. Cautiously he made his way over, leading his draught deer. We watched anxiously, for this seemed the only spot where a fairly shallow crossing was possible and if we could get over without a soaking from this ice-cold water we would be very relieved. I sincerely hoped we should be as lucky as we had been with all the other streams that had begun to open.

The snow and ice seemed to hold Nils well enough, and he came back for his sledge. Slowly he began to walk back over the snow bridge, and the loaded sledge, drawn by his deer, swung away from the safety of the bank and over the fast-running water.

Suddenly, what we had dreaded happened. With an explosive crack and a dull thud the bridge collapsed. Nils, the deer, and the sledge were all thrown into the swift flow. Nils struggled up, soaked and panting, grabbed the head of the deer, which was still attached to the overturned sledge and managed to cut it free from its harness. The deer plunged forward to the farthest bank and shook itself violently.

Our whole concern now was for the overturned sledge. Aslak and Josef plunged into the freezing water to help Nils, and the three of them managed with much panting and straining to draw the sledge out on to the other side. The bindings round the load had held firm and had even tightened from the wetting, so not too much harm had been done.

We now had to throw over a long line to the men on the far bank and allow our sledges to be pulled through at the shallowest spot. Then we had to follow.

As I stepped up to the thighs in the icy water the shock was so great that it completely took my breath away. Somehow or other I was dragged across by the rope, soaked to the waist and numbed with the cold. Anna, who knew the danger of freezing feet and legs, immediately pulled off my breeches and footwear as fast as her capable hands would allow. She then rubbed my feet in the snow and hit them hard until they were red and sore and the warmth began to flow back. She gave me a pair of Lapp leggings from her sledge, which I pulled on gratefully. With some dry sedge grass wrapped round my bare feet in the skallers, I was none the worse for the soaking. The Lapps, too, had all been changing in this way, using fresh, dry grass to replace the sodden mass round their feet. Now all was well again, and we were once more on our way.

The last night's travel was soon upon us. I had no accurate way of judging where we were and the Lapps did not require a map, for they knew from long experience every aspect of this landscape. When one has no real idea of exactly where one is, distances and time seem much longer. They certainly had to me, but now Nils came and sat on my sledge and drew with a stick in the snow. He showed me how close we were to our immediate objective—Komagfjord, and even I could understand that we were near, by the general excitement among both the caravan members and the reindeer. The big herd could sense and smell that they were approaching the water of the fjord and they increased their pace accordingly.

I was feeling tired and was as red-rimmed round the eyes as the Lapps were, from the bitterly cold air and the smoke from the fires. Nils knew I was a bit done-in, for the snatches of sleep during the bright light of the day were a poor substitute for real rest. He tried to cheer me up.

'Wait until you see Seiland over the water, Brandon. Every year I wait for that sight. Tonight as we are travelling along we will tie a line from your sledge to the back of Anna's and you can sleep as we go along. We have a very heavy day tomorrow with no chance for the usual sleep.'

He said this with a smile and a little nod over to where Anna was packing for the night's travel. She turned and gave us a big wide grin. It was certainly true that she spoke very little to me, and seemed even more shy than little Anna-Maria, but she kept a watchful eye, and was always ready to spring to help if I was in trouble. What a grand couple they were and what good companions, even if the conversation was very limited.

That evening the sky was again very clear and the air cold. I settled in the furs on the sledge and did, in fact, doze off into a sleep that must have lasted several hours. I felt safe in the knowledge that Anna would not let my reindeer stray from the trail.

When I awoke the dawn was again in the eastern sky and the sense of burning in my eyes was much less. I felt rested and when Anna turned and saw I was awake she indicated by pointing several times ahead rapidly that we were nearly at the last ridge before Komagfjord.

It was soon bright daylight, with the promise of a warm day. Snow blanketed the whole of the plain thickly, but our progress was fast, as the night had been very cold, and the surface crisp and firm.

It was at that moment that the first of the pregnant deer calved. We all knew that there was a great hurry to get the herd over the water as soon as humanly possible, for the signs of the imminent calving were plain, and the number of calves safely born was of the greatest importance to the family, financially.

Aslak was with the herd, cursing softly to himself, because two of the females had just begun to drop their young. They had rolled about in the snow in the moments before starting to give birth, and were now both standing with the small hoofs of the calves sticking out from under their short tails. There was nothing for it but to keep them as quiet as possible, and to hold off the dogs, for the reindeer always likes to be left alone in peace when calving. This was indeed an unfortunate time for them to choose, just before the edge of the plain was reached.

For some time they stood straining to give birth, then suddenly the small, wet and bloody forms of the calves shot out into the snow. There the two youngsters, one pure white and the other a warm brown, lay steaming in the air. The two females, released now from their labour, turned and began to lick quickly at their offspring with their big rough tongues. The snow was stained red with the afterbirth.

Soon the youngsters began to show signs of wanting to rise from the cold snow. With quivering thin legs, they tried to stand, took a couple of uncertain steps forward, and then fell headfirst into the snow again. With great energy the does continued to lick and gently nuzzle them until once again they struggled to their feet. With widespread legs they managed to push forward, helped by their mothers, until at last they found the warm milk for which they had been instinctively seeking. All the while they were drinking, the does went on licking, with hard rasping sounds, until the soft fur of the calves was clean and almost dry.

At the right time the newly born reindeer would have been greeted with all the pleasure of every fresh arrival in the spring; but now they were a problem. They were too small to totter along and over the edge of the plain, down the steep slopes to the valley below. Aslak had to pick them up and put them on one of the sledges, and in doing so he tainted them with the human smell; the last thing the does liked at that time. He cursed again, but there was nothing else he could do.

The six hundred, or so, reindeer were now visible ahead; bunched together, with the herders on the flanks. The dogs were barking furiously, for they, too, could smell the water, and even I felt the difference in the air. The breeze was now strong, whereas for most of the journey across the plain there had been a great stillness. After a few minutes' travel there was a shout from Aslak ahead and Anna turned again and gave me another big smile. I knew full well what she meant. We had made it.

A new sense of being alive flowed through me and the excitement I felt was like that of a child who is in sight of a promised treat.

The herd paused and as we caught up with them we stopped our caravan of sledges. I walked to the edge of the plain and looked down with Nils and Anna. Behind us lay the limitless, or so it seemed, white Vidda or plain, and now we were able to gaze over at the valley far beneath us; at the dark blue water of the winding fjord, and at the long strung-out line of little wooden houses that made up the small fishing-settlement of Komagfjord.

The sun seemed to catch the water with a million sparkling points of light. It was one of the most welcome sights I had seen for a long time, and in the distance rose the tall rocky slopes of Seiland, still snow covered. It was to this island that the reindeer were to be taken for their summer grazing.

The copses of birch saplings made patchwork patterns of warm sepia against the white of the snow on the slopes beneath us. Still there was no sign of opening leaves, but the buds were waiting and would burst out quite suddenly when they were ready. One of the marvels of the north is the way that the spring arrives, as it were, overnight and one wakes to a dawn when all the leaves have miraculously opened.

Far below us and to our right we could now see the little pier jutting into the water and three fishing-boats, looking like toys, at the end of it.

It was a picture of quiet calm, but after several minutes of admiring the view, I began to wonder how on earth we were to get down to the bottom, several hundreds of feet below. There appeared to be no trail, and huge boulders and jagged rocks pushed up through the snow in many places, showing how dangerous it was going to be.

The reindeer herd now split into groups and began the descent, moving swiftly and surely through the groves of young birch trees. They were led by a truly magnificent beast, who pushed and plunged through the deep snow, ahead of all the rest. It seemed incredible when Nils assured me that the deer knew exactly where they were going, and there would probably be no accidents, as they had been down this great slope many times in the past. The trail through the trees was there, even if covered.

We watched them for a time, with the dogs trying desperately to keep up with them, but sinking deep into the snow on their short legs. On the right flank Josef moved on skis.

At long last we saw the whole lot assemble at the bottom of the valley, and pause for a few moments.

It was the sign for our party to get moving. The caravan of sledges was led by Anna, holding her own deer at the head of her sledge, by a short line. Little Anna-Maria sat on a pile of furs together with a young deer that had been injured on the journey. I was to follow immediately behind her.

I must confess to some trepidation at the thought of getting down this perilous unseen trail with my own packed sledge! But it had to be done, and I put my faith in the sturdy form of Anna ahead of me. Behind me came the other sledges, and when I turned I saw Nils giving me an encouraging nod of the head.

'Just follow Anna and don't worry,' was his final advice before we plunged over the edge of the cliff. I saw Anna's sledge disappear and summoning up my courage, I followed in her wake. I could feel the head of my own reindeer pushing into my back. I was supposed to be leading *it*, but it was, in fact, propelling me from behind. Fortunately it had no antlers! Slipping and sliding as I went, I was being forced downwards.

I saw that Anna was moving ahead quite unconcerned; she was, in fact, following a natural cleft between the snow-covered rocks that made a trail over which the caravan could move. It was probably the only place where this was possible, and it showed the immense value of knowing the terrain so intimately.

My own deer pushed its big splayed forefeet deep into the snow to act as a brake, for the heavy sledge was behind it and down we went with me hanging on to the animal for support! Anna looked up and gave an encouraging wave as she sped down. In what seemed like seconds later she had reached the bottom and was standing on her sledge on the level snow in the valley. Little Anna-Maria was still seated in her place on the furs, happily oblivious of the dangerous descent.

Thankfully I reached the bottom, following in the trail that Anna had left with her sledge runners and deer. She patted me on the shoulder, and Nils and Berit were down behind a few moments afterwards.

Aslak came down last on the snow-scooter, which he handled with much skill, and also pride.

Well, we were down. The caravan formed into a small circle, and Nils got out his pipe and sat down for a quiet smoke. He was never in a hurry, and he knew that he had much to do for the rest of the day, so he would take it easy for five minutes.

Aslak busied himself by fastening two sledges behind the snow-scooter and setting off towards the village, his dogs barking beside him. He would arrange by telephone for the arrival of the 'pram', or big flat-bottomed craft that the Lapps would use for the transport of the deer over the cold water of the sound to the island of Seiland.

So many deer had been lost in the past by drowning during the swim over that Aslak, in common with other herders, had formed a Reindeer Breeders' Association for their common good. It had been arranged that they hire a former fishing-vessel and this large old flat transport, that had probably been a landing-craft during the Second World War, was ideal for carrying about two hundred deer at a time over the water.

Aslak was far from happy about the dangerous and difficult rocky slopes of that part of Seiland over which his own herd of reindeer would roam all the summer; but he had no chance to change the area, for this was the grazing-grounds allocated to him and to Nils.

Of Ole Gaino and his wife and sons there was now no sign. They and Elsa and the baby had left us on this final day and had travelled off to another point of land further along the fjord, where there own reindeer would assemble for the crossing. But for the actual trek it had been far better to travel in one big group from the start, and so it was that they had all kept together for as long as possible.

Nils and Anna took their sledges, after their short rest, and began to climb another path that led upwards to the heights on our left and on the other side of this valley. The big herd were already up there, followed by Josef and several dogs, and there they would remain for a time, waiting for the signal that the 'pram' had arrived. The snow was so deep that both of them sank up to their waists as soon as they got between the trees, and they had a very hard and tiring time pulling their sledges up behind them. The reindeer dragging the sledges panted and strained, and sank. The weight pulled them down, and the Lapps had to work very hard to make any progress until they reached firmer ground.

At last, with us watching them quite helplessly from the valley beneath, they turned and waved, and then were off at a better pace to remain with the herd until we met them again shortly.

It was now that Berit and I had to make our way to an old wooden hut, close to this trail, and in which a girl called Hannah was to be waiting for us. Hannah had made the long journey from the heart of Finland up to Hammerfest. From there she had taken the fjord steamer down to Komagfiord. Berit seemed very cheered at the thought of meeting her; she was a good and very capable helper for the summer.

CHAPTER 7

Hard Night's Work before the Crossing to Seiland

SMOKE was rising from the chimney as we approached the hut, and as soon as Hannah saw us coming she was out in the snow with a big shout of welcome.

We entered, and then looked at each other. The hut was filled with the smell of fresh rye bread and rows of newly baked loaves were on the table. Hannah was busily preparing for the days ahead. She was fairly tall, well built, with as fine a pair of legs as I ever saw on a woman. Her hair and eyes were dark, and the set of her jaw strong and determined. She was not a woman to trifle with, I thought.

She and Berit began a very fast converstion, and Berit's high-pitched laugh was frequent. We sat and drank coffee and ate some of the delicious fresh bread. It tasted better than anything I could remember at that moment.

Hannah could speak a good deal of Swedish, which was to be a great help to me, especially later when it came to dealing with old Fru Sara, the head of the big family, who we were yet to meet. She was to prove another worthy companion, even if she greatly preferred the company of Berit and her merry laughter to my own for most of the time!

Ahead of us lay a cold and difficult task, which the men left to these two capable women. Later in the afternoon we made our way to the small pier, where Berit had the immensely valuable assistance of Arne Anderson, a tough Norwegian fisherman who was determined to make Berit his wife if it was humanly possible. He was not finding it easy to get her away from her nomadic way of life, however; but he was trying, and had already commenced building a house in the hope that she would accept him.

He was the owner of a solid boat which was a great help to the family all the summer in many ways, but now he added his strength to the task of loading up big rolls of fencing wire into a smaller boat, driven by an outboard engine. When we had filled this, leaving just enough room for us to somehow find a place between the rolls, we were ready to set off from the pier along the fjord, which lay before us as calm and quiet as a mirror in the evening light. The big snow-covered sides of Seiland were reflected deep in the surface until the waves from our boat broke the still water. It was certainly very cold in this small open boat, but Berit and Anderson kept up a cheerful chatter, and he for one was glad she had arrived for another season.

The island rose to our right as we moved along and the village and pier on the edge of the fjord on our left grew smaller until we finally rounded a bend and it disappeared from sight.

Ahead of us, on our left, and almost clear of snow at the bottom, was the point of rocky pebbles on which we should land. This was the 'nose' from which the reindeer would be taken over to the island by the 'pram' when all was ready. Behind the natural beach of small pebbles precipitous rocky slopes rose until they reached an impressive height. Deep pockets of snow covered the rocks, and Berit looked at it all with some misgiving. The snow was so deep and also soft that it would make our task far from easy. The wind was bitingly cold, and we had the cheerless prospect of spending a night in the open on this exposed in-hospitable point that jutted into the fjord.

Anderson lifted roll after roll of heavy wire on his back and dumped them on to the level rocks at the edge of the water. His duty was now finished, and we saw no more of him.

We followed Berit ashore with a few poles and the tent cloth, as it was necessary to put up some sort of shelter for the night, however rough. We chose a level patch of rock free from snow about a hundred feet above the fjord. From here we had a clear view, so that when the fishing-boat and the 'pram' did arrive we should quickly see it.

Opposite to us, and seeming quite close, Seiland loomed. It looked a very dangerous craggy place, to my inexpert eyes, for deer to roam, and Berit said they lost a good many each summer due to broken legs.

The snow was frozen hard in the bitter air, and after a warming cup of coffee made over another smoky twig fire, Hannah and Berit began the thankless job of unrolling the wire. They then dragged each roll over the snow so that it could be twisted round trees and old posts left from the previous years to make a fence. This was an extremely hard task, and even with the firmer snow the women sank to their waists as they drew the wire upwards behind them. The fence was to enclose a large area stretching from the edge of the water and rising steeply upwards, following the natural lines of the rocks.

Poor Hannah was now reduced to crawling over the snow, the end of a roll in one hand. Hands quickly became numb in these conditions, and as the wind rose higher it was getting even colder and more miserable. At two in the morning, I admired them greatly. My job was to try to unroll the coils of wire and get them as flat as possible, but I felt I was not the help they should have had by a long way.

A herd of reindeer can break down a very strong fence, so this one had to be built firmly enough to hold them when they came down the path from the heights above.

The women were now soaking wet on both arms and legs, as they tried to fix the end of the fence into the freezing cold water with stones. It was then necessary for Berit to go along its whole length down the path that the deer would follow, to test its strength.

Suddenly, much to my surprise, Ellen, the daughter of Nils, who had been with her father and Aslak and the big herd far above us and out of our sight, had decided to come down to help us, even at this hour in the early morning. She knew, of course, exactly where we would be.

Eventually we crept out of the piercing wind into the shelter of the small rough tent and made another fire. Even the smoke seemed bearable after the cold. I think I have never felt so completely chilled right through my clothing.

At three in the morning, with the sky a metallic gloomy grey, Ellen had a strong desire to master English, of all things. 'I love you because . . .' She had learned that phrase, and at once both the other women laughed loud and long as though we were on a picnic on a summer day. One felt that such women could hold their place in a man's world at any time.

We had no real idea of when the boat and 'pram' would appear, but Berit thought she heard the deep 'chug-chug' of the engine, and at once began to pull down the tent. It was important that when the deer came down we must not be in their path or they might move to the right or left in the wrong direction and make nothing but trouble for the herders. The pathway down was very narrow and winding, and had been used for generations, but it was essential that the deer came in one long line and kept to this route.

One cheering spot of colour in this wilderness was the golden upright catkins of the sallow, pushing their way up from the snow on tiny dwarf bushes. It was early May and whatever the weather the yearly cycle of life must continue.

As we had now no tent, Berit said we must move about quickly to keep warm, and this was certainly true. It was getting lighter, with the promise of a fine day. The greyness was disappearing and the sun just rising. The water of the fjord was slowly becoming bathed in soft yellow beauty, and the snow on the island of Seiland glowed with spots of bright fire as the rays of the sun caught peak after peak.

Berit began to burn patches of heather, which crackled with clouds of acrid smoke. This did not seem to worry her, and to feel the warmth better she lay down by a big rock, curled round like a dog, and pulled her red plaid shawl over her head. We could hear she was asleep in a few moments. What a woman, I thought!

I also tried her game, but the smoke always seemed to curl round into my face, and in the end I sat by a rock and gazed out over the water, cursing at the boat for keeping us here in the cold.

As we waited the welcome sound of the engine, far reaching in the quietness, came to us from round a bend, and after another few moments we saw the slow-moving boat, with the big black craft drawn behind, at the end of a long line. Our waiting period was over at last.

The boat stopped close to the rocky beach from which our fence rose, and began to manoeuvre the landing-craft into position so that the end with the ramp, that would be let down, came right up to the stones. At last all was ready from our end for the final act of the long trek to begin.

Suddenly I was left quite alone. Berit and Hannah went down and rowed out to the fishing-boat, and Ellen had made off to go back to help her father with all the sledges on the heights above us.

14. Berit and Hannah preparing the *skaller* or winter moccasins.

15. Nils Sara preparing the reindeer skin for making the *skaller*. Strips of birch bark are laid on the inside of the skin to dry it.

I wanted to find a good spot for filming the operation; for this was an essential part of my educational film, but it was not so easy. I had to climb higher with my camera, tripod, and another bag round my shoulders, and with only a slippery path a few inches wide for my feet. I looked down, and far below me was the water, blue but icy cold. One false move and I would be in it. No one had time to worry about me, that was certain.

Carefully inching along, with a sheer precipice beneath me, I reached a snow- and ice-covered rock surface, overlooking the beach below, where the herd would gather. I waited there, holding my breath, for something to happen.

At long last I saw high above me several figures that looked no larger than matchsticks. Shouts reached down to me, and in a moment I saw the first of the reindeer appear over the ridge some hundreds of feet above, and led by a small figure that I knew must be Nils. For a moment he paused, then he slowly began to descend the path. The big bell hanging from the neck of the leading deer was clanking and inviting the others to follow. One by one they did so, and soon there was the thrilling sight of a long line of these reindeer, with their pale winter coats hardly visible against the snow, making their slow way down the very steep slope to the flat patch by the water's edge.

Shouts from Aslak and Josef on the flanks grew louder, and I sensed the whole ancient drama and also natural beauty of this scene that had been enacted for so many centuries.

Nils and the leading deer were down, and then the big fine animal went to the edge of the water and stood gazing steadily over to the island. It was quickly followed by the others, until eventually the entire huge herd had gathered without any fuss. Standing or lying, they waited for the next move. They seemed to know that this was the start of the season at their 'Promised Land' and they appeared very quiet and contented.

In the heart of the herd, and lying on the stones, were the two new-born calves. As I watched they rose on their spindly legs and began to search for milk, but on every hand they were met with rejection, tossing of heads and snorting from the adults. The smell of Aslak, who had handled them on the way down, was strong on them, and neither the mothers or any of the others would accept them.

Aslak told me they would have to be killed, and the fine soft skins used for clothing. It seemed a cruel fate for these lovely small creatures with their large and pathetic eyes. But there was no time for sentiments of this kind, as all was now ready for the loading of the first deer on to the waiting 'pram'.

CHAPTER 8

At Last they are Over

USING long strips of hessian, the Lapps now began to build two lines of fencing, to guide the animals up to the flat bottom of the pram. This was the critical moment of the whole operation, and each of the party was ready for almost any action that the reindeer might take.

Young Anna-Maria, thickly wrapped in furs and shawls, sat quietly watching in the snow, close to where I was standing. The dogs were tied up close to me also, and this they bitterly resented. They kept up a furious barking, much to the annoyance of Aslak and Nils, who shouted at them many times. My own dog seemed to find satisfaction in sitting close to me feet, however, but his every muscle was strained with the effort of remaining there and not jumping in among the deer.

Many times I spoke soothingly to the dogs, who ignored me, but this was one time when the herders did not need them, for the space in which the deer could move was very small. If a wild panic had started the herd could easily have dashed up the slopes, and perhaps broken through the fencing that Berit and Hannah had erected. It would have taken a good deal of time and effort to have rounded them up again.

When the lead-in fence was ready Nils again took his place with the leading deer, this time standing close to the entrance to the 'lane'. Holding the deer by a short rope from its neck, he started to move and the bell clanked again. The idea was that the whole herd would quietly follow the two of them into the 'pram'. On paper it sounds simple enough, but in actual fact it took about two days before the whole of the six hundred or so animals were transported over.

All was now calm and quiet, and the Lapps were silently stationed at various points round the herd waiting for what would happen. Nils walked up the ramp and the clanking bell sounded encouraging. But this time, unfortunately, the herd were in no mood to obey its call.

As soon as the herders began to drive the animals behind the leader, they all sprang to sudden panic-stricken life. Wheeling round in sweeping circles in the small space they had, they ran in crazed groups, with Aslak standing helplessly in the centre, trying desperately to divert them from this rotating action.

Berit, Ellen and Nils had been waiting hopefully at the entrance to the 'pram', ready to pull the deer up, but Hannah, Anna and Josef had now to spring in all directions, waving their arms and shouting, and doing everything possible to stop a dash through the flimsy fencing that the women had built in the night.

The deer showed all the fear and stubbornness of animals who were naturally afraid of walking up a gangplank, in the same way as I have seen pigs behave on an English farm. The Lapps were becoming very hot and exhausted, for the sun was rising and the day was getting warm. But they never lost their good humour; and after a great deal of persuasion, the first few deer were forced up the ramp and pushed into the rear of the 'pram'. There they could be shut off, for the vessel had been divided into two parts, each capable of holding about a hundred animals, by a gate across its centre. Little by little this rear part became full, and at last the gateway was closed off and at least some of the herd were now safely aboard. But what a small result after so much hard work.

I had been watching Berit from my distant perch overlooking this thrilling scene, and in between filming I had been filled with absolute admiration for the way she had been fighting in the centre of the deer. Her thin frame seemed incapable of standing up against these terrified beasts; but she had fought, held legs, and pulled and struggled in the very heart of the mob. At any moment I expected to see her trampled underfoot, but she survived, and now had a moment to look up at me and give me a cheerful wave.

'Would Cox like to have a go now?' she shouted, and the men also looked at me with dirty faces but wide grins, and asked if I had taken some good film. Despite all the work, they were really enjoying themselves, this was the amazing fact. I could imagine the grumbling from a normal group of workmen doing such a thankless job, but these Lapps were almost making a game of it, hard as it was.

At last, after about another hour, the second half of the 'pram' was filled, which meant that about two hundred of the six hundred we had on this pebble shoreline were loaded.

The two solid Norwegian fishermen who were in charge of the boat pulling the 'pram', had been watching the operation keenly all the time, and now they slowly edged it from the shore and into the deeper water of the fjord. The ramp at the back had, of course, been lifted up, and the vessel rode quite easily in the water despite its heavy load.

Ahead of it lay a journey of about four hours, for they would travel around to the other side of the island, where the land was much flatter and better for the animals to be released. The ramp would then be lowered, so that the animals could swim the very short distance to the shore.

We stood and watched the vessels as they grew smaller in the distance, and soon they had rounded a bend in the island and the sound of the engine grew fainter.

The Lapps now had a break for some hours, and with much enthusiasm Berit began to light a fire, for they were all hungry and tired, and in need of hot food and a few hours' rest.

Snow-water filled the battered kettles, and heedless of the thick smoke the whole group gathered close to the flames, relaxed and thankful to lie on the rocks for a time. There were no words of complaint from any of them, and the whole thing was taken as part of a day's work.

'How would Cox like to have a go at the next loading?' Berit asked again, and they all burst into laughter at this. It probably did sound humorous to them, thinking of me chasing the deer and fighting to get them on to the 'pram', and I joined in the laughter. One thing I had quickly learned from my travelling with these people was that to be able to laugh at oneself was the best way of making friends with them. If I had tried to be on any sort of dignity, then it would have been hopeless. They did not mind my helplessness, which they found amusing, as long as I laughed at it as well. They thought I was worse than Anna-Maria at times, I am sure. At least that is how I felt!

Two-thirds of the herd were still left on the shore. They had settled down again to a calm waiting and would be no trouble for a time. Aslak and Nils caught, with their lassos, several of the young deer who were still without the cuts in the ears that denote ownership. Throwing them down expertly on the rocks, Aslak cut the set of marks with his knife to show that he was the owner. This marking is very important, and I was to hear and see much more about it in the future, especially when we came to the big autumn round-up.

The hours passed all too slowly for me, and I was still extremely cold after the night. I had had none of the exercise that the Lapps had had, so that my body and feet had not warmed up at all. I was glad of the warmth of the dogs which curled around our legs. Anna, Berit, Hannah, Josef, Nils, Aslak and even little Anna-Maria all kept up a very cheerful conversation in Lappish, which was beyond my understanding, of course, but they tried to make me feel warmer. Berit and I rubbed hands, and I wondered again how her small, thin hands were capable of such efforts.

Ole Gaino, his wife, and sons were not now with us, as they had left earlier on the trail to join up with a group further down the coast headed by a tiny, gnome-like Lapp called Per Kemi. Lapps are not usually tall, although they do have a fair proportion of tall men among them, but Per Kemi was about the smallest little nomad I ever saw. He and Ole Gaino owned deer between them, but they had to have their own summer range, of course, and could not mix their deer with those of the Sara family.

I rather missed Ole Gaino, and told Berit so. Also Elsa and the baby, who had travelled with them on the trek. To my surprise, Berit jumped up and asked if I would like her to take me by boat to where he had his herd waiting for the 'pram' to be free. I could stay with them for a while, and travel over with the deer with them, and then rejoin the Sara family later.

It sounded a good idea, and her energy amazed me. Soon we were springing down to her boat, which had a very troublesome old motor. After a lot of patience and effort, it was started, and we chugged away down the fjord, waving back at the group we had left.

After a couple of hours travelling close inshore, we came to the rather cheerless and flat spot where Per Kemi and Ole Gaino had their deer. I was landed there and after a hot drink of coffee, Berit left again.

Ole was glad to see me, as was Karin, and also Elsa, but I did not

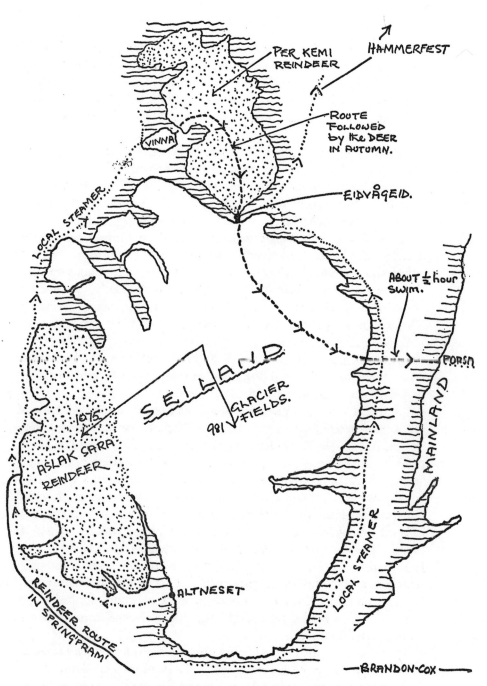

THE SUMMER GRAZING GROUNDS

think that Per Kemi was overjoyed. He hardly greeted me at all, and I understood him, for I was a stranger to them, and really had nothing to do with his group. Lapps, like others of this world, do not take kindly to people they do not know and who seem to be poking their noses into their business. It was as simple as that, but I was glad that Ole felt differently.

The contrast between the Sara family and these people was great. There was an air of poverty about everything they owned, and even their deer looked thinner and weaker, in addition to being far fewer in numbers. Life for them was, in fact, really hard, but the good humour was there, nevertheless, if one could get behind Kemi's reserve.

I told Ole all that had happened, for Lapps like to know news in great detail. It would be some time before the 'pram' would reach them, I added, so they would have time to clear their own possessions up a bit after the migration. Their deer were standing very quietly, enclosed by a big circular fence close to the edge of the water. They were grazing on what vegetation there was, for the snow had left this flat area.

I could at least relax here inside the Gaino tent, warm myself by their twig fire and have hot stew, which was very welcome. I had not been warm for many hours and one is apt to stiffen up very much in long periods of such continuous cold.

I studied Per Kemi, hoping he would not notice it too much. He was the most wizened-faced Lapp one could hope to meet. Very small of stature, but tough of character. His nearly white hair stood out like a sweep's brush round the top of his head, and he seemed never to be without his pipe between his teeth. I suddenly thought of a way that I could gain his friendship a little. I still had a supply of tobacco, brought out from England for this purpose, and a packet was with me in my jacket. I went over and offered it to him. He looked with his keen eyes into my face for a minute, then broke into a wide grin and held out his hand to thank me for the gift. He opened the packet, smelled the contents, and then cleaned out his pipe and filled it with the English mixture. He drew on this, and it was obviously much to his liking, for he looked over at me, nodded his head several times, and seemed in much better humour after that.

His wife seemed to be his perfect mate. She was so thin and small as to be hardly visible, with a sharp face and a shrill way of talking. But I found she was very tough and capable, and they had brought up children who were a credit to them. One of their daughters, another Ellen, a girl of about nineteen, was quite charming. She had a rosy face and big eyes, and despite all the trek and hard work, they had just experienced, still managed to look neat and clean.

Per's son, Mikkel, a strong, tall young man, did not like me at all, that I could see. He was on leave of absence from the military to help his father, and resented any foreigners. He was a rather restless character at that moment, for the life of the Army—in which the Lapps have to serve for a period as well as the Norwegians—had opened his eyes to many things that he felt their primitive way of life denied them. I could well see his point of view, of course. He could speak good Norwegian, and could have conversed easily with me, but kept out of my way. Ole Gaino apologized somewhat for him, but I understood his attitude very well.

We waited in quite good weather on this charmless point of rocky land by the edge of the water, until at last we heard the welcome chug of the fishing-boat engine, and saw in the distance the boat and the 'pram'. I wondered when the two men on it had last slept. They certainly had not had time for it since I last saw them. However, they still seemed in good spirits when we greeted them, and this time, much to my surprise, there was very little trouble in getting this lot of deer on to the conveyance. I imagine it was because Per Kemi was so much a part of the reindeer life in his appearance that they naturally followed him without question. That is how it seemed at any rate, and the first two hundred of their herd were soon away on the much shorter journey to their own grazing-grounds.

All went well with the next group, and as these were all they had, it only remained for us to load their mass of poor possessions on to the deck of the boat. Sacks of clothing, pots and pans, mattress covers filled with an assortment of items that hardly seemed worth saving to me, poles, personal chests, wire, and then last the snow-scooter of which Mikkel was the proud owner and driver. The dogs and children came next, and then at last the rest of us all found a place, amazingly enough, somewhere on the deck of this fishing-boat, and we were set and ready for the trip.

Per Kemi looked smaller than ever on the boat, but he was still in charge and wanted to show it. His tiny wife locked herself in the small galley, from where in a short while she had warm food cooking and coffee boiling. Her nose was quite red, and her tiny arms looked very white when she appeared with sleeves rolled up, but I felt a glow of friendship for her. She soon called us all to a meal of frozen fish cakes, warmed in the large old frying-pan over the galley stove.

The little galley was filled to overflowing, and it was impossible for the whole group of us to get in, so we sat outside, surrounded by furs, for the air on the water was always icily cold to the face and body.

From their roomy blouse-jackets the herders drew loaves of bread, from which they cut huge chunks with their knives, which are the universal maid-of-all-work for the Lapp. Into their coffee they dropped thin slivers of dried reindeer meat, and from their worn rucksacks came containers of margarine and other items. No one minded an amount of dirt and reindeer hairs on food. Hairs always seemed to cover every-thing. They were a nuisance at times, but one was soon used to pulling them off bread, margarine and other food items.

Ole seemed to me thinner than ever in his tight skin leggings, and without his thick white winter cloak. Every time he looked at me, which he did repeatedly, he had a wide grin, and his pale blue eyes had the habit of gazing at me almost without flicker. His face seemed even smaller, surmounted by a brown leather hat with ear flaps. We could not converse very much, but there was a feeling of friendship which was very pleasant.

The men and also the women settled down between piles of skins and began rolling their cigarettes, getting out from their blouses their packets of papers and packets of tobacco for this purpose. They like a smoke, and this is the cheapest method.

When last they all had had a proper sleep I did not know, but now, after the food, the whole group began to settle into a quiet mass. Ellen, Kemi's daughter, curled herself into a ball, a dog at her head and shel-tered from the wind in the prow of the boat. She pulled a blanket over her head and was quickly asleep. Her brother Mikkel settled himself on the seat of the snow-scooter, leaned over so that his head was resting on his arms on the handlebars, and was also soon asleep. Ole Gaino, Karin, the boys, Per Kemi and his wife, all pushed themselves deep into large roomy sleeping-bags made from reindeer fur, and the only sound now was the slapping of the water against the sides of the boat and the front of the 'pram' behind us. The reindeer made no sound.

I went into the small cabin of the boat. The captain, old John Nilsson from Alta, handled his load with a humorous look in his tired eyes.

'We manage to sleep about once a week at this time,' he explained in answer to my query. He then asked if it was Saturday or Sunday, as he lost all track of the days when moving the deer, he said. He and his partner, a squat, solidly built man with a square face lined with the years spent at sea, cod fishing in the icy waters of winter, had been away from their base now for fourteen days, with only the shortest of rests. But when the reindeer arrived at the coast it was a matter of working all round the clock for these men to get the herds over to the summer grounds. Rest was a luxury that had to wait.

The boat and the 'pram' were partly state-owned and partly owned by the reindeer owners, and were booked well in advance by each family. The exact date of the Lapps' arrival at the coast was a matter of guess-work, however, for everything depended on the weather, and two or more families could find themselves waiting for transport at the same time with all their deer. He did the best he could, he said, and I could well believe him.

John Nilsson was over seventy, and fifty of his years had been spent at sea. He seemed to carry a constant joke in his mind, for there was a twist to his mouth that showed a ready humour. I could just about understand his thick dialect Norwegian. As we slowly continued on our course, we talked about the difficulties of the nomadic Lapp life and how much easier it was for normal farmers who could remain in one spot.

His boat had also weathered more than fifty years of the northern storms, and had the feeling of a vessel that should be pensioned off. Like its captain, however, it refused to give up working.

The low-lying coastline where we were to release the deer loomed closer. It was time for the group to stir and get ready. Ole Gaino and Mikkel lowered a small boat and rowed to the end of the 'pram', where they lowered the ramp.

Reindeer are good swimmers, and for centuries it had been their habit to swim across to their summer grounds from the mainland, but this was certainly a much more efficient and more economical method of transport for the Lapp herders.

The boat stopped, and the 'pram' gently swayed up and down at the end of its long line. With the ramp opened and the men standing inside, the leader of the herd stood for a moment looking over the water at the coast. Then it plunged into the water, and group after group jumped after it. Swimming easily and gracefully, they reached the rocks in a very few moments, shook themselves vigorously, and with an un-hurried gait began to move inland without a backward glance. They would now break up into small groups, and it was the last we should see of them, as a herd, until the autumn.

CHAPTER 9

Old Magic Drums and Cures

THE flat swaying transport vehicle was now empty, and a sense of relaxation flowed over those of us still on the boat. With a deep chug of the engine, the vessel continued with its human load round several more bends until we came to the small quayside of Eidevageid, which was where the Kemi and Gaino families made their summer camp.

A huge towering mountain rose behind the village as a backcloth, and only a few scattered wooden houses stood on the flat rocks close to the water. It did not look very inviting.

There was much work to be done and little time to examine the surroundings, however, for the whole of the possessions of the two families had to be lifted up to the level of the pier. We used a very ancient wooden crane for this, and very soon there was a big pile of clothing, furs, sledges and all the rest. Last of all, came the snow-scooter, which would be used to pull the loaded sledges high up to the primitive wooden huts which the Lapps had made themselves.

It was very gloomy and blowing cold when all was ready. The financial business had been transacted in the cabin, and had taken some time, as the families were poor and there had been a deal of haggling over the price.

Skipper John Nilsson shook his head rather sadly at me when we were under way again, back along the fjord. He had a good deal of sympathy for the Lapps, whose way of life was not the romantic image that is often depicted in colourful tourist cards. The life of the nomads was tough indeed, and only their sturdy sense of humour and independence made it appear easier when one was travelling with them. It was this ability to take all situations in a light-hearted way, making the best of everything, that had always enabled the Lapps to survive in a world that had given them nothing freely.

I had a firm feeling of friendship for Ole Gaino, but was glad I was not to remain at this spot. The point of my journey had been to see how the transport went and to watch the deer swim to the shore; also to pay a brief visit to the quayside to see the unloading.

We were soon heading back for Altneset, further along the coast of the island, where the Sara family would now have arrived.

The sunlight caught the tops of the hills, bathing them in a rosy glow that made them glitter. The wind was bitterly cold, however, and blew the snow from the peaks in showers of misty white.

The warmth of the cabin was very welcome. It served as a mess room, and also as sleeping quarters for the two men. As I sat there, the squat solid form of the mate came down the small hatchway, and he inquired: 'Do you like boullion with reindeer meat?' With some enthusiasm I replied that this would be more than welcome, as it seemed a long time since I had had a proper meal.

With efficiency that had come from long experience, he busied himself with the potatoes, one large onion, and a meat bone. These, together with several other ingredients, which he handled very lightly, considering his huge hands, eventually produced an excellent hot meal. At this time —it was now eleven at night—such food tasted better than any that could have been served at the finest hotel. After eating my fill, I felt considerably better. I had to refuse his coffee, however. It was much stronger in its bitter blackness than my stomach!

At about 12.30 at night, with the light outside still very bright, we reached the other small pier that led back to the insignificant group of houses forming the fishing-village of Altneset. High above this was to be my home for the summer, sharing it with the Sara Lapps.

We stopped the engines close to the pier, and the men tied up the boat. We were all very tired, and within a few moments had turned in to sleep, for many hours, in the small warm cabin; whilst outside the light grew brighter and brighter as the morning sun lit the snow.

When we rose again I remembered that we did not have all my possessions with us. I would have to go back with the boat to Komagfjord, where the long trek had ended, and to the hut from which Berit, Hannah and I had begun our journey to the headland. This was a great nuisance, as it was a long and difficult walk through deep and soft snow, up a very steep path. However it had to be done.

When I finally reached the hut, to my surprise I found Hannah still there. She had been waiting for me, it seemed, and very glad of her company I was, for there is something reassuring about people who know just what they should do in all circumstances, which was more than I did at times.

I had hardly arrived when suddenly a fierce storm blew up, and for several days it snowed and blew, making all thoughts of travel back to Altneset impossible. However, we had food, and could cook in the hut, so we were safe until it passed.

Hannah in the meantime had developed rather bad pains in her arms, after her very cold and wet hours at fence-making, and it was her idea, as soon as we could, to visit an elderly Lapp who had the reputation of healing by touch.

Lapps have always been very superstitious, and in the old days they had their private places of sacrifice in many parts. In 1673 Schefferus illustrated in a woodcut how a *seide*, a stone or wooden idol, was worshipped. The seide was placed on a bed of twigs within a semicircle of reindeer antlers, and the Lapp approached it with bare head and on his knees.

Here and there, although very seldom now, a seide can still be found. Generally the place chosen had some significance to the Lapp family, either from its atmosphere or because of some experience they had lived through at that spot.

In these far northern districts it was formerly common to divide the world of gods and spirits into higher and lower regions, and this is shown in the ancient and now discarded magic drums.

Living as they had always done so close to nature, the Lapps naturally adopted the sun *Peive*, and the moon *Aske*, as important gods, and among other signs that were drawn on their symbolic drums were, *Tiermes*, the God of Thunder; *Biegg-olmai*, 'the wind man'; *Vaeralden-olmani*, 'man of the world', who was thought to bring luck to the reindeer; *Rananeida*, a female who represented spring and the period of growth; *Leib-olamai*, 'the blood man', who ruled over the wild animals and was god of hunting, and *Tjas-olmai*, 'the water man', who controlled the lakes and fishing. There were also a large number of important spirit-beings that represented 'the woman creator', 'the spinning woman', 'the door woman', 'the bow woman', and another who 'permitted shooting'.

Together with the nature gods, the Lapps also had a number of deities of a more abstract nature. The supreme god was *Jubmel* or *Ibmel*, clearly identified with the Finnish *Jumala*; and among the Swedish Lapps, *Radien-attje*, 'the original father', occupied the same role.

The ancient Lapps, of course, lived in a world that was filled with far greater dangers than today. Storms, illnesses, wild animals . . . all were connected in some way with a spirit world. It was necessary to enter into this world of the spirits to obtain peace, and this was achieved through the use of the magic drum.

Every Lapp family had its drum, with its sheet of reindeer skin tightly stretched over an oval wood frame, and covered with symbolic drawings. Real magic power was possessed, however, by only a few of the Lapps.

One who was thought to be really expert was known as a *noaide*, 'wise man or sorcerer', and he was the Lapps' *shaman*.

They did not have any special costumes, like the shamans of the Siberians, but they did have a belt from which was hung the magic charms and symbols used when performing with the drum.

The drum of the northern Lapps, the bowl type, was widespread from Finnmark in the north to the Pite district in the south. The skin for this was stretched over a wooden bowl which had two or more perforations. It was usually calf-skin, and held to the frame by sinew threads, or even rivets of bone or wood. The figures were painted on the skin by using the red dye of the alder bark, and even today, when one sees one of these very old drums, it is amazing how well the dye has lasted.

There could be as many as a hundred figures painted round the edge and over the surface, and trinkets of silver, brass and copper were often hung on leather thongs, bound with tin thread, from the frame. Small bones with magic properties, such as the penis bone of the fox and bear, the teeth and claws of the bear, and others, were also hung from the drum. The drumstick was usually a Y-shaped hammer of reindeer horn, ornamented with delicate carvings.

16. Fru Sara displays the finished *skaller*, watched closely by the author's hooded crow.

17. Mikkel Matis was eighty-six and the oldest member of the big group. He was still active, and could spot the reindeer without glasses.

It was by using the drum that the *noaide* could fall into a trance which could well last up to twenty-four hours. His spirit wandered into a far-off world and achieved great things. In this state he could meet the gods, and discover the whereabouts of a lost reindeer herd, or find a cure for a certain sickness that was worrying the family. In *Savio*, the other world, there were a number of sacrificed animals to aid him in his wanderings—a reindeer buck, a bird, and a fish, on whose help he could call, or whose form he could assume when he was in danger and had to cover great distances quickly.

Usually, the noaide returned from his visit to the spirit-world with his mission successfully accomplished, but it was thought that if he was not successful he might never recover from his trance.

The Lapps also consulted the drums for knowledge of the future. For this, a triangular piece of reindeer horn, a ring, or even a bundle of rings, were placed on the skin, which was then hit by the hammer. The vibrations caused the horn or rings to move towards certain of the figures, and from these positions the future could be prophesied.

Eventually, through the wanderings of the missionaries, the *Samer* were converted to the Christian faith, and the old drums were ordered to be destroyed.

The drums that remained became dispersed over Europe by collectors, and in the Nordiska Museum in Stockholm there is a fine display of these ancient relics. Probably there are others still well hidden away, but I never managed to find one during my wanderings with the Lapps, and all my inquiries were met with a negative answer. It was probable that they would not tell me, in any event, as I was a foreigner; and it was only by the greatest patience that I had managed to gain their confidence so far.

In Norway, it seems that King Christian IV was the first to make a serious attempt to introduce Christianity to the Lapps, and after a visit to Finnmark, he issued a decree of capital punishment in 1609 for Lapps who refused to give up their old beliefs. It was in 1691 that orders were given for the building, at Varanger, of the first church especially for the Lapps.

Thomas von Weston was the Lapps' own apostle during the first half of the eighteenth century, however, and he worked among them with great effect, and to great and useful purpose. Knud Leem, who was the author of *Description of the Finnmark Lapps*, published in 1767, and *Lexicon Lapponicum*, in 1768, was to be his great successor.

At the beginning of the nineteenth century the priest Lars Levi Laestadius was the important influence, and it was his form of Christianity that most of the Lapps eventually adopted. One feature of his type of religion is the strong sense of excitement that can build up during a gathering, and it can be explained by the fact that it has something of the shamanistic ecstasy about it, and forms the basis on which the religion is built.

Of course, it was never possible for the wandering nomads to go to any regular church services when they were converted to this form of Christianity, but special days during the year became holy and festival days, and the times of the big markets were arranged to coincide with these festivals in places. Then the colour and attraction of the Lapp costumes can be seen at their best, for most of the clothing is brilliantly coloured, and seen at a festival or Lapp wedding it is something to be remembered for a long time.

. . . Hannah was now most anxious to pay a visit to the old 'troll' Lapp—one who was supposed to be able to heal by touching and stroking the injured or painful part of the body. As soon as the weather cleared so that we could get out of the hut, and despite the deep snow, we decided to trudge as best we could along the trail that led to the fishing-village. There, in a fishing-home where he lived with relatives, we found old Johan Albert Johanssen Carlssen, over eighty, but still healthy, if somewhat vacant in his expression. It was the 17th of May, and a day of great rejoicing in the north, for the Norwegians were celebrating their Independence from Sweden, which they obtained in 1814. Patriotic songs were being sung everywhere, and at the small school at Komagfjord I later joined the youngsters in a march, when the Norwegian flag was proudly carried along the route, with the singing groups glad of the warmth of the sun, for this special day, despite the snow in some depth all around them.

But for the moment we were concentrating on Hannah's aching limbs, and were glad that old Carlssen could see us. He shook Hannah's hand and then mine, and accepted with pleasure the tobacco I had brought him. His eyes were red-rimmed and his mouth completely toothless, which gave him a comical appearance when he laughed. He was small and a mixture of Lapp and Norwegian, which he thought gave him extra strength. His father had been a Norwegian fisherman and his mother a Lapp. I found this was a very uncommon blending, as the Lapps liked to keep their marriages in their own race as much as possible, and mixed alliances of this sort were not encouraged at all.

I think I was the first Englishman he had seen, and he regarded me with as much interest as I looked at him. He carefully felt my face with his fingers for some reason, muttering to himself for a time, and nodded his head. He asked Hannah several questions in a thin, high small voice, which I could not understand, then looked hard at me again. I began to feel I was in a doctor's surgery, and tried to give him a smile to show friendship. It was some time before we could get him to come to the point of treating Hannah's arms. First he wanted her to tell me something of his own life. He was very glad to have the chance to talk, that was obvious, and liked to remember events from the past. He had hunted foxes and game birds, and recalled, as far as I could gather, that not since the time the Russians had attacked Norway, and had been beaten back by the weather, many freezing in the snow, had he seen snow so late and so deep as this spring.

The light was only dim in the simple room where we sat, and as he swayed back and forth in his chair, talking away in his singsong voice, I became sleepy and could well understand how the Lapps could so easily fall under the spells of the ancient *noaides*.

He asked Hannah to remove some of her clothing, then gently felt her arms, which he stroked several times, muttering and swaying all the while. Then he pulled at each of her fingers in turn, and repeated the whole performance again. I feel that we would have believed him whatever he told us at that moment, and when he eventually said: 'Thats all. You will feel much better tomorrow', we were both ready to accept his word.

I could see Hannah was much impressed and also more cheerful at once, and we sat and chatted, or at least I listened to the strange tongues, for some time, whilst the sun sank and the temperature again dropped sharply. We drank coffee with him and his relatives, who were fisherpeople themselves, and wanted to hear as much about England as possible, and especially about Winston Churchill, who was their great war hero.

We left the house, and the old man, at midnight, walking back along the path deep in snow. The wind bit deeply into our faces, but the

lovely midnight sun coloured the fjord water with a soft peachy glow
that made the cold bearable.

The next day the snowstorm swept back over us, and it felt very
depressing. I began to think longingly for the spring days in England . . .
Maytime with its blossoms and warmth . . . here we had only deep snow
and bitter cold.

However, outside the hut, in a tall birch tree, two hooded crows had
their nest, and all day we watched them defending it against the pair
of ravens that patrolled this valley. Their deep, resounding calls echoed
through the trees, and at their approach both the crow parents would
spring into the air, harshing, calling, and pursuing the ravens until they
left them in peace.

I found them fascinating to watch, but now, after this last night of
storm, when we looked from the hut window in the morning, the tall
tree was down. Uprooted by the wind, it had fallen, and the nest was on
its side. There were no sign of the parents, but I was determined to go
and find out if anything could be saved. I made my way, through the
soft snow, and in the big well-made nest, lined with a mass of small
birch shavings and sheep wool, found one youngster, hanging from the
side by one of its legs, which had become entangled in the wool. It was
not dead, and began calling loudly when I touched it.

Gently I released it, and brought it back to the hut, where it sat, a
poor, half-frozen object, obviously glad of the warmth.

What to feed it? That was the question now, as we hoped to keep it
alive. I found some sort of answer by visiting a near-by Norwegian, and
digging a mass of small worms out of a manure heap, from which we
had scraped the snow.

The crow swallowed these at great speed, and then settled down in a
'nest' that I had made for it in a cardboard box. Well, we had added to
our responsibilities, and I only hoped that we could feed this small bird,
who was now so dependent upon us.

How can it be possible, I asked Hannah, that the slender silver birch
trees and the willows are still bare of leaves? It seems extraordinary that
the days are going so fast, and yet the weather is still so bad. An old
farmer had assured me that the spring would break out overnight when
it did come, but now it will soon be summer, I thought, and spring will
have passed us by without us having noticed it at all.

Yet there were signs . . . the starlings had returned to the north, and were nesting noisily in boxes put up for them on some of the fishermen's wooden barns. It was quite remarkable the affection that these starlings seemed to arouse with the local people so far north. To us in England, used to seeing them in their teeming thousands in the heart of London, it is difficult to imagine that when they return in small parties to the north of Arctic Norway in the spring they are warmly greeted and encouraged to build close to the buildings. And I, too, found that their noisy wheezing and squawking was a welcome sound, although it made me miss home very much.

At midnight Hannah and I sometimes saw the thick reddish coat of a fox passing through the trees close to our hut. In the light of the northern light it was clearly visible, and would stop for a few moments, sniffing and watching the hut. The foxes here were of remarkable size, and their fur very thick and close. They had few enemies and grew quite large.

Signs of wildlife were to be seen and heard all around the hut, and in the still-naked birch trees the lovely little willow tits uttered their high, thin 'Zi-zi-zi' as they searched for insects that had already made their appearance on the warmer days. With their sooty black crown, white cheeks and brownish coat, they seemed so alive and vital that it helped to dispel the feeling that summer would never come.

Another welcome bird, and a bright splash of colour, was the wheat-ear; they are certainly not afraid of cold. When they flew from the stones near the hut which was a favourite perch of a pair, their white rumps showed plain, contrasting with the black tail; they could never be missed. The male had for his breeding dress a blue-grey back, with black ear-coverts and wings, but the female was less striking in her attire. This pair were shortly to have a nest under some of the stones, and every time we came now from the hut, their harsh calls of 'Chack' were heard.

Huge magpies' nests, too, could be seen in the trees around the small isolated farmstead near the hut. Each spring these dashing black and white birds which are such a feature of the north added to their numbers until, at times, they reached quite enormous proportions. It is strange how the magpie, suspicious bird as it usually is, seems to like the company of humans for its nesting in the north. They had gathered in large groups for the winter and I once counted as many as thirty chattering together in one tree, waiting for the weather to improve.

Other charming small birds that were a real symbol of these northern lands were the snowbuntings. They would rise like clouds of snow-flakes from among the birch twigs, where they had been almost invisible, with a plaintive 'Teup' and a 'Tsweet' and then settle again quite close.

The fjord ended close to this hut at Komagford, and a dashing and brilliant bird that again reminded me vividly of the east coast of England in winter was the oystercatcher, with its black and white striking form and the long red beak. One or two were to be seen along by the edge of the water among the rocks, and at my approach they would fly swiftly, showing stout pink legs, and calling 'Kleep, kleep, kleep' in alarm so that it echoed a long way over the water. In the fjord when it was windless, they were reflected with great clearness, as were the eider duck that would nest in scattered groups or possibly alone around the water's edge.

Hooded crows were never absent, and I often watched them at work searching for food along the water's edge. They had the habit of turning over stone after stone systematically looking for food under-neath. There was a great intelligence in all their actions, and my own youngster whom I had christened Charlie, when he recovered from his shock of near-death, was to develop and show all the high intelligence of this species. Many miles indeed was this bird to travel with me, and to become a very close companion.

Hannah felt much better immediately after her visit to old Carlssen. It was probably because she firmly believed in his powers, but whatever the reason, it was a welcome fact, and meant we should be able to travel as soon as Andersson could take us in his boat to Altneset, where we were to rejoin the main Sara family group.

The weather changed to clear brightness again, and one day, with a blue sky above us, we took all our possessions down to the small pier. Amongst the gulls screaming around the long rows of drying fish, we loaded them on the deck of Andersson's *Kristine*. We were glad indeed, after our enforced long delay, to be on the move again, and to be joining up with the family at their summer camp at Altneset. It already seemed a long time ago since the reindeer had been transported, but with the greatly improved weather—at least for the moment—we set out, with Andersson in good spirits at the thought of seeing Berit again.

CHAPTER 10

The Hut between the Rocks

THE wind had dropped, and the journey to Altneset became a series of dramatic and beautiful vistas of mountains receding into a blue distance ahead of us. The formations, still with snow on their peaks and driven into the crevices of their hard granite sides, seemed to change their patterns from moment to moment.

I thought with admiration of the hard work the Norwegians had put in in their efforts to bring electricity out to this lonely part of the world. Carried by double poles over these forbidding mountains, and then, when it reached the fjord, carried by underwater cables to the other side. It seemed indeed remarkable that any country with such a long coastline could have managed in such conditions as are experienced here in the winter, to maintain the service. I became very friendly with some of the tough men who were out working on these lines in all weathers.

We eventually arrived at Altneset after a trip that I will long remember for its scenic grandeur, and when we drew up at the small pier Berit was there to welcome her Andersson, who greeted her with a bear-like hug. Their courtship was rather amusing, but it was greatly frowned upon by old Fru Ellen Christine Sara, the head of the spreading family, who I was now to meet.

We managed to drag all our possessions to the end of the pier, and then up the twisting, slippery slope that led to the plateau, high up behind the rocks, on which the Lapps had their summer camp. The view from here was magnificent, and one could understand their liking for this position.

Hannah helped me put up my own tent, which I had brought out from England for the summer, and Berit showed us a flat place that seemed the most suitable, as all around us was swampland that would never give any dry ground for the tent. Her spot had a lovely outlook, along the fjord, but I viewed it with misgiving, for it was completely exposed to the weather, and I wondered what would happen if we had more bad storms.

However, I eventually erected the tent, placed in it all my possessions, and then joined the family. There was to be no rest for them that evening, however, for a local wedding was being held in one of the isolated farmsteads, and from many parts guests had assembled, arriving by boats, which were now in a line around the pier below.

Berit and Hannah had been invited, and there was a great deal of activity in the makeshift old hut that the Sara family used. It was extremely primitive, but served better than a tent, and in another shed by the side of the fjord water Berit had stored and hung all her valuables.

The clothing the two women wore for the wedding was indeed a riot of colours. Blue costumes, heavy with many yards of thick material in the pleated skirts, were highly decorated with many rows of braids, all containing different patterns.

They were watched over by old Fru Sara, who regarded me with no great liking in her eyes. She was some seventy-six years, and a wonderful example of the older type of nomad Lapp. Strong and active, and with hands that could still twist the reindeer skins and oil the autumn footwear, she ruled over her family in a stern manner. Although her eldest son, Nils, was now over fifty, he obeyed her in all matters, even though he himself had many children.

The woman has always held a very strong and important place in the life of the Lapp family, and upon the death of her husband she assumes the place as head of the family, however widespread it may be. She is obeyed in a manner that is very impressive to watch.

When we managed to converse a little, the old lady told me she also had ten children, most of them having been born on the trails, and in the old tents.

She regarded my crow with great amusement, and her face creased into one of the rare smiles that she sometimes gave to me.

'I can well remember when I have thrown the afterbirth from one of my children to the crows for food,' she recalled, and saw nothing strange in this recollection. Her grey hair was well combed, and there was a strength of character about her face and appearance that I have not seen before in any Lapp.

When we set out for the feast, for I had more or less invited myself out of curiosity, the two women wore at their throats the very lovely and quite valuable silver ornaments that are so cherished by them. When we arrived at the home of the Norwegian couple the Lapp women certainly looked the most colourful in every way.

We were given glasses of grog to drink, followed by a large variety of the Norwegian open sandwiches, coffee, small glasses of liqueur, and then the very rich cream cakes which are a speciality of the north.

There was a good deal of laughter and attempts at talking English, followed by dancing and much toasting with spirits.

The house was on level ground close to the fjord, and behind it in the distance the hills rose in a half-circle. They were still plainly visible despite the late hour, and it was possible for the whole party to dance in the open air. The newly married couple stood in the centre of the dancers, whilst a big circle moved one way and then the other around them, singing in their honour. It was delightful to watch, and all were in a good mood because the drinks had not been neglected for a moment.

At one o'clock in the morning I walked back alone towards the tent. I did not know how eventful the rest of the night was to be!

It was very cold, but still so light that only by looking at a watch had one any real idea of time. I turned in, thankful of my sleeping-bag lined with eider down. Feeling warm and pleasant, I began to fall into a welcome sleep.

An hour or so later without warning, and utterly unexpectedly as far as I was concerned, a howling gale of wind and rain hit the tent. One moment all had been quiet, and the next the tent was shaking, as if it was going to tear to pieces at any moment. The sides blew in until they touched my face, and everything began to heave in the most alarming manner. This was not the worst, however, for the force of the rain was directly hitting the entrance, and soon it began to force its way through the material. A pool of water gathered around the central tent pole and began to spread out. I tried to draw on as many clothes as possible amid the confusion, and mop up the water with a cloth as fast as I could.

Meanwhile, Charlie the crow was screeching his alarm and anger from his place in a plastic bowl in the tent. The noise of the rain and the waves of the fjord water hitting the rocks below made all thoughts of further sleep impossible, and I had to work hard all through the night defending my belongings from the inrush of water. How bitterly I regretted having put my tent up in this exposed position, for what I had feared had happened on the very first night.

Somehow the night passed, and my head felt as heavy as lead when the wind dropped and the rain subsided in the early morning.

Thankfully I crept out into a grey, miserable, cold world, with heavy clouds hanging so low around the tops of the mountains that it felt possible to reach up and touch them.

I looked down the fjord and saw the hut of Nils Sara, a very poor affair, from which smoke was rising from the pipe chimney. I was standing thus when he came to the door, saw me and waved a welcome. He was a most friendly man, with kind and intelligent eyes, and always ready to assist, as he did at this time.

There was no continuing to live in my tent, that was clear; and the problem of where I was to go was solved by the Lapps suggesting that I take over a deserted and terribly battered wooden shed belonging to the Gaino family.

This was quite close to where my tent had been standing, and for the rest of the day Berit and Hannah worked with a will trying to clean some of the coating of thick dirt that covered the floor, and blocked the old iron stove in the corner by the door. I was more than grateful to them.

Nils, too, helped me to move all my equipment from the rain-soaked tent, which was now in a state of collapse, and eventually Hannah, with some dry wood from the Sara hut, made a fire in the old stove, and the place began to warm up. It was the first time it had been used for ages, and cobwebs of dirt hung from every beam. It was impossible to hang anything up until we had cleaned round a little, but soon we had fastened some reindeer skins to the walls, and with a few boxes for seats and one for a table, it was almost like home!

Hannah then made us all a meal of boiled cod and potatoes, and I felt that it would be possible to improve my new home with a little effort and a few tools.

The hut had two small windows, and the site was truly magnificent. The view from the rear window took in the whole length of the fjord below, from which, sometimes late at night, it was possible to watch the small fjord steamer. It was our only link with the outside life as it slowly moved towards the pier of Altneset. The boat was lit by many lights, which reflected deep in the water, and gave it a festive appearance. Even more so as the music on board from a radio carried far over the water to us in the still air between the mountains on either side.

At the back of the hut was a swampland, for which one needed rubber boots, covered with a mass of thick, fluffy cotton-grass, which made the ground look as if it was covered with snow in the middle of summer.

Brightly coloured flowers of many sorts were now appearing between the cracks in the rocks, and in every possible patch of suitable soil; and on the rising ground that swept up from this swampland, every birch tree suddenly and dramatically appeared to have a shimmer of light green.

The ice and snow was now melting and began to pour down the side of the rocks. This was to be our water supply, and although it was beginning to run with force the Lapps said that if the summer was dry it might quite possibly dry up altogether. We managed to place a piece of piping into the flow, to carry it into a big wooden tub. This was constantly filled, and from it we could obtain bucketfuls without too much effort, apart from getting over the very swampy ground which sucked at the boots at every step.

A slippery path led to the fjord and the pier, which although it was right below seemed far away as we were so high up. My hut was built on the only flat piece of rock in the area, between huge boulders. Pieces of wire had been thrown over the roof and attached to large rocks to keep it on in stormy weather. The whole place looked as if it would fall to pieces in a strong wind.

I was to spend many hours with hammer, saw, nails, and driftwood I found along the fjord side, making it more habitable, and I found the task a pleasant one. The sense of this far-away freedom, and the un-reality of the whole way of life, began to impress itself more and more upon me as the days were to become weeks and the summer to gradually pass into the beautiful autumn.

From the hut I could see along the fjord to the scattered wooden fishermen's houses that formed the small community, and to the post-house. There was one small shed close to the pier, which was opened twice a week for a few hours in the morning, for the sale of food, and during these welcome opening times, the primitive shop was always filled with either members of the Lapp family or the local Norwegians. It was possible to buy all the main essentials: flour, sugar, margarine, cheese, apples, potatoes, and various spreads for putting on the bread, and even tinned meats, so we were not so badly placed as we might have been.

This shop was a source of supply for my furniture for the hut. Wooden boxes, when they could be obtained, made me shelves and places for my books and cameras and other items that must be kept clean. Very soon it was in such good condition that old Fru Sara began to pay me a daily visit in the middle of the morning, sitting and waiting whilst Hannah made her coffee. The two would talk and laugh for long periods in Finnish, which was impossible for me to understand, and Hannah would afterwards translate as much as she could remember.

The old stove in the corner had a large crack in one side, through which we could clearly see the fire. The whole structure was immensely dangerous, but as we had no other, we made it as fireproof near the roof as we could.

Wood for the stove was a problem. It all had to be found along the fjord side, and carried up the slippery slope to the hut. It needed two people, for most of it appeared to be old railway sleepers, which were extremely heavy. They had to be cut up, using a big tree-cutting saw that Aslak owned, and then chopped into suitable sizes for the stove. It was hot and tiring work, but it had to be done, and many hours went into this labour during our stay at the coast.

The worst days were when Hannah decided to make bread. There was no bread to be bought, and all the Lapps made their own. I must say it was some of the best bread I have ever tasted, made on that old, broken, but still workable stove; but the wood it needed for a week's baking took me all day to gather and saw and chop.

On such days the interior of the hut became so hot that it was impossible to remain in it at all. We could not open the small fixed windows, so the heat could only escape through the open door. On a hot day it was like the interior of a furnace, and I had to admire Hannah's pluck in sticking at her bread-making in such conditions.

I went over one day, as soon as the hut was in some sort of presentable condition, to visit Nils, and found him resting for a while, sitting in the sun on a high rock with his small, blonde daughter Anna-Maria by his side. They were a devoted couple, and he was an excellent father.

When I came to the hut Anna, his wife, was working on her knees beside a big pile of matted reindeer hair, spread out on the grass. This she was pushing into sacks, for sale at 6 kroner (about 6 shillings) a kilo, to a factory where it would be used for filling mattresses and pillows. It helped to give them a small income, together with the unwanted reindeer antlers, which they also sold for about 4 kroner per kilo.

Nils was mending his fishing-nets when I called on them, he had his own row of drying fish, covered with net to protect them from the gulls. Fishing has always played an important part in the economic life of the Lapps at the coast. Formerly those of them whose life was spent by or near the fjord waters made great use of sheep- or goat-skins for clothing. making them waterproof with applications of fish oil. Money was always a big problem, and although they traded with merchants, selling them salmon in exchange for goods they needed, an old account from 1638 shows how badly they were treated by the buyers. They were forced to pay taxes, and for this they had to perhaps kill off the few livestock they possessed.

It was because of this treatment that trading with Russian ships that called at the coast became attractive and popular with the Lapps. From the foreign sellers they could obtain linen for sails for their small boats, cloth, ropes, hemp, copper and iron, nails, axes, and so on. Also they were provided with flour and grain, which was essential to their well-being. For these goods they exchanged dried fish, so plentiful from the sea along this coast, and furs.

The Russian vessels would come to the coast and along the fjords and remain for perhaps a month, during the summer. This trade, valuable to both sides, was sadly missed when it ended because of the First World War. The coastal Lapps, like the Norwegians, were able to cut a small amount of hay for the cattle they might keep, but the living was hard and uncertain and depended so much on the weather. They had no fast, well-built boats for deep-sea fishing, of course. For the Nomad Lapps the fish offered a welcome change of diet, and also saved their precious supplies of reindeer meat.

Nils later pushed out his boat, about the size of a large rowboat, very wide, and with an outboard motor, and we went out for a short distance to fish. The water was so clear that we could see the large cod swimming lazily directly beneath. The sunlight penetrated deep into the fjord water, and in the shallows grew a jungle of moving weeds with long green tendrils.

Fish after fish was quickly and easily pulled up. We used only a twisting, bright, flashing bait and could even watch as they snapped at it. It was almost too easy, and we were able to return to the camp after a couple of hours with a good load of large cod and several of the firmer and more tasty coal-fish.

We sat later over a steaming bowl of potatoes and cod, which Anna had quickly prepared for the family gathering, which was now quite large. There were Nils, Anna, Josef, Ellen, Anna-Maria, and three other boys I had not met before, but who had been sent out from school to join the family at the coast: young Nils aged nine, Aslak ten, and Mattis eleven. I could never understand how they all managed to fit so well into the very primitive and small hut, every night. But the Lapps have the power of being able to sleep easily under nearly all circumstances, and pile together all round the walls. The larger of the two rooms was always quite neat, and Ellen was usually to be found there all the summer, with a huge pile of dirty washing in a big old bath, or a pile of bread dough being rolled. The washing methods left much to be laughed over, for the water was so much trouble to obtain in large quantities from the waterfall that she had the water in her big wash bowl nearly black most of the time. However, they were cleaned, the shirts and the underwear, in a grey manner, but in time the greyness became darker and darker, for they were never really properly rinsed.

It took all her time, together with the milking of the goats they kept for their precious milk, to cope with such a household. She was not helped so very much by her mother, for Anna and Nils often went off together in his boat for days, in search of the reindeer as they roamed freely in the heights opposite us on the other side of the bay.

'Tell me something about the castration of the male reindeer in the autumn, Nils,' I asked after our meal, when we were gazing over the water, watching for signs of the animals through our binoculars.

'I can tell you one thing, we want nothing to do with those clippers that some of the families use these days. There never will be any better way of castrating a deer than with the teeth. There is no risk of in-fection, and it can be done in a few seconds. Of course, it takes good teeth and not everyone can do it, but you will see in autumn how easily it is done. And none of our deer lose any weight after it either. They are in better condition than ever for either selling or pulling sledges.'

'How many does it take to castrate a deer?' I asked.

'Well, first the animal has to be lassoed, and then if it is a big buck it takes perhaps two or even three of us to drag it down, turn its head on one side and hold it ready. Then perhaps Mikkel will do the castrating. He springs down quickly between the back legs and bites through the cords. We have to keep the animal from twisting too much with fear, but it feels little otherwise. It is over in a minute and then we jump back and allow it to get up and rejoin the others. It quickly forgets all about it, but Mikkel has a lot of hair to get out of his mouth, and he needs plenty of drink that day. When there are a lot to be done it is not so easy for him.'

We sat, and whilst Nils quietly puffed at his pipe, with Anna-Maria by his side, the nets gently moved in the slight breeze and the drying fish swung back and forth. He took everything in his life with the deer so calmly, and there was always a feeling of strength about him that was reassuring. His face was deeply lined, but his eyes were bright and friendly. The hard life they lived made all the Lapps appear older than their years, but on the other hand they were far more elastic in their movements and ways than the normal town dweller.

Nils broke the silence suddenly. 'I am going to have electricity laid on to my hut as soon as they bring it to that new house they are building along the fjord.' This was an amusing statement, I must say. How on earth they would ever pass his hut for electricity I could not imagine, but later on he proudly showed me the wires and the lighting and in some manner he had managed to persuade the Norwegians to do the work, and to do it cheaply. That much was certain, for he had little money for anything.

Of all his children, Nils was probably proudest of Josef. At fifteen he was a quiet, deep-thinking boy who had a good head. Nils got out his latest report from the school at Masi and showed it to me, whilst his keen eyes kept watching my face.

It was an impressive report: SG (Special), MG (very good), G (good), and NG (quite good) in all his subjects, with MG predominating.

I asked Josef to come over to my hut and show me his Norwegian examination papers. He did so willingly, but rather shyly. We sat together in the evening glow of mysterious light, with the remains of an old Lapp tent behind us, and the crow perched on my sawing-block, gazing over the water, as was his habit. I felt at this moment that I was now part of a life that it would be difficult ever to leave.

18. Anna, the wife of Nils Sara, and their son Josef on the island of the Artic Terns. Boiled in the old coffee pot the eggs proved very tasty.

19. Harvesting the sedge-grass in August. When dried it is used to line the *skaller*.

20. Anna-Maria feeding the author's hooded crow.

21. Ellen Sara, daughter of Nils, and Anna-Maria with the family's goats.

22. Nils, Fru Sara's oldest son, and himself the father of a large family.

23. Fru Ellen Christine Sara water-proofing a pile of newly sewn *komag*.

CHAPTER 11

Island of the Arctic Terns

JOSEF was a rather reserved good-looking boy, with deep brown eyes. He had never said very much on our travels, but now, sitting with me alone, he began to show a surprising sense of humour, and was ready to talk on all matters to do with his way of life. He was one of the boys who still showed a real eagerness to follow in his father's footsteps.

When he produced his examination paper in Norwegian I could see that, wisely, the questions were all directed at finding out how much the youngsters knew of their own culture.

I have the questions before me now, and I found them very interesting.

1. Spring migration. Explain why this takes place and what work is done on the actual migration. What is the work at the summer camp?
2. Write how you would tell a tourist about Lapp daily life at work and school.
3. You have travelled with the boat along the Kautokeino river. Write what you saw on that journey.
4. Write a letter to a relative and describe what has happened since you last talked together. Remember that he would like to know how you have got on at school.

These, surely, were most intelligent questions, as they forced each Lapp child to concentrate on his everyday living. The answers had to be written in Norwegian, which they now all learn at school.

The very ancient Lappish language was still spoken between the

Sara family on all occasions, and I found it was almost impossible to learn. It is very rich in words and expressions that refer to reindeer breeding, fishing and hunting, as one would expect. It is when we come to the machine age that difficulty is found with the finding of suitable words and phrases.

The old language belongs to what we call the Finnish-Ugrian group; this consists of nine languages, of which Lappish, Finnish and Hungarian are probably the three that most influence the language of the people of the north.

Together with Samoyed, these nine form a main group called Ural languages, after the Ural mountains.

The connection between Finnish and Lappish is not so close as to allow a Lapp to understand Finnish, as a Norwegian can understand Swedish, for instance; but the Lapps certainly find it easier to learn Finnish than any other language.

There are a large number of Finnish loan-words in the Lapp tongue, and vice versa, and in northern Finland there are many Lapp words. But the Lapps have also taken words over from Norwegian and Swedish, sometimes in the most primitive of forms, and the language generally has preserved ancient features of other cultures in this way.

I found it amazing that the old nomadic Lapp, Fru Sara, could speak several different languages, but in some way she had taught herself, and she could converse easily in Finnish.

The Lapps, spread over a very wide area as they are, have developed many dialects, and these can differ so greatly that a Lapp from one area cannot understand a traveller from a distant region. Those who speak northern Lappish cannot understand the southern dialect, but now it is becoming more and more common for Norwegian or Swedish to be spoken, so there is really little difficulty in being understood.

The use of their own language is something that has sustained the Lapps up to the present day in their contacts with each other, and the Radio of the North has daily news in Lappish, even though the number of these ancient people is comparatively small.

Josef, like all the elder sons, would later have to serve a term in the Norwegian armed forces, together with the young Norwegians. This of course, widens their outlook very greatly, and also makes it necessary for them to have a knowledge of Norwegian.

We talked long, and it was late when Josef left me. The crow had returned from a last flight around the hut, to sleep for the night on my stick, which I always placed in a corner for it. He had the habit of flying off at about five in the morning, and rousing the Lapps in their hut by constant pecking on the windows , and cries for food. He knew that there was always food to be had there, and I would not see him again until later in the day.

Charlie was proving an amazing and very intelligent pet. He was not confined in any way, but although there were an enormous number of crows around he would have nothing to do with them, attacking any fiercely who came too close to the hut. With me he was the model of good behaviour, and liked nothing better than when I sat to write up my daily notes. Then he would perch on my shoulder, and settle down, closing his eyes, and showing every sign of pleasure. He was always so with me, but would attack all the Lapps with vicious blows, especially Hannah and Berit, who were the ones who really treated him best!

The Lapp dogs soon became completely used to Charlie, and accepted him wandering around their legs without any fuss. He would sometimes even steal a piece of meat from between the feet of one of them, who would look up in surprise, but never seemed to mind. They just looked upon Charlie, who Hannah always called 'Pirri-pirri-poo', as a bit of a nuisance who had to be tolerated. . . .

The weeks went by, and once more the weather had changed, after a few sunny days, to greyness. The dismal, low-hanging clouds made visibility along the fjord almost nil. I had been affected for some little while by a rather bad stomach upset that made it necessary for me to see a doctor.

Now, this sounds very simple in our civilized life, but it was quite another matter here. I found that people had to be really ill before they called on a doctor, for the nearest was at Hammerfest, a long boat journey up the fjord, or in desperate cases they could call on the flying-doctor service.

This consisted of a plane, with floats that could land on the fjord waters as close to the patient's dwellings as possible. From the plane, the doctor would be rowed to the shore by one of the fishermen, and then he would attend the patient in his home. It was seldom I saw the flying-doctor service in action, for the people were very fit, but now and again the drone of the engine could be heard in the distance, and the small silver plane winged over our heads.

I decided to take the boat along the fjord to Hammerfest, and on a sullen, grey day, even though it was late June, I set off in one of the small steamers that make this regular run from Alta day and night, summer and winter. Without these steamers the people of the villages would be completely cut off, for there were no roads leading from one settlement to another. At Altneset, for example, without a boat one would be stranded.

We reached the town at nine in the evening, with a cold rain falling, and I found a comfortable and warm room for the night, and was up early in the morning, to visit the local hospital. This had a feeling of informality about it, with just a young and charming receptionist and a good-looking young doctor who came out to meet me. He gave me a thorough general examination, eventually saying that he thought the attack would pass over in several days, for which I was thankful.

We began to talk about the medical services for an area such as this. He had had a year as a district doctor, he told me, in one of the very outlying regions, and said they now had ten doctors at Hammerfest, which was too small a number. This is a problem that the whole of this part of the arctic north, whether it is in Sweden or Norway experiences —a lack of sufficient doctors.

In the late afternoon one of the fjord steamers was leaving for Alta, and I was able to travel with this, much to my relief, for the northern town of Hammerfest seemed very dismal in bad weather, despite its newness.

The Captain of the *Marøy* spoke excellent English, and I spent some time with him on the bridge, where I greatly admired the Decca Radar. This, he explained, was wonderfully helpful, especially in the darkness of a winter night and even in the sunless daytime twilight of the winter, and in the fogs that at times sweep along the fjords.

That evening the clouds hung lower than the tops of the mountains on either side of us. It was cold, too, and not in the least like June. I was always aware here that I was in the far north and the coldness of the wind made winter clothes welcome on such an evening.

All along the route from Hammerfest to Alta there were small villages to call at. Post was exchanged, and goods delivered that had been ordered from the town. Now and again a passenger or two would alight.

It was not until after midnight that we reached the small pier at Altneset. My hut, perched high over the water, could only be approached by a slippery rocky slope. From the water now we could see that a yellow light shone from the window. It was welcome to know that there would be warmth inside, even in the land of the 'midnight' sun.

Hannah had left a fire burning and a pot of water stood on the stove making a cheerful steam. The crow woke up immediately I entered the door, and flew down to my shoulder. He rubbed his strong beak gently against the side of my face, missing my eye by a fraction of an inch, but I was never worried about that. This same bird that would hack out the eye from the head of a dead reindeer could be as gentle as a feather when it came to touching my face. In all the years I have wandered in the fields and woods I have never before seen such an intelligent bird.

I sank down on the pile of reindeer furs which formed my mattress. The life was making me thinner than I normally was, but the next morning I felt cheered and strengthened by the sight of a brilliantly blue cloudless sky. What an immediate difference it made when those depressive clouds lifted.

It was just the day, with the air fresh and clean, and the sun sparkling on the water, for a trip by boat. I was glad indeed when I saw Nils waving up at me from his hut—my own was the highest of all the huts.

I went down. 'How would you like to come on a fishing-trip and collect a few sea-birds' eggs as well? You should be able to get some good pictures,' he said.

Nils did not have to ask me twice. He had talked to me of the Island of the Arctic Terns, where the family went by boat at certain times in the summer to collect some of the eggs for cooking. They did not do any wholesale robbing of the nests of this lovely, graceful bird, but treated it more as a day out with some food thrown in, free of cost. On such a day as this it was a perfect opportunity, for the eggs would soon all be hatched.

Two boats were necessary to take us. In the first went Nils, Anna, Josef and Anna-Maria, whilst I was towed behind in another, borrowed from Aslak. All the Lapps owned a boat, of sorts. It was essential to them during the summer months, and was left behind at the coast in the autumn.

The bright sun reflected back with a hard glare from the mirror-like water. On the still snow-pocketed slopes, rising up to each side of us, reindeer were to be seen in small groups. The big herd had split up for the summer, and those we saw now had darker coats than the very pale, almost white, fur of the winter.

The scene was dramatic, and a perfect background for the Lapps in their patched and worn, but colourful, clothing. As we moved at a fairly good speed, the sound of the outboard motor had a jarring loudness in such stillness. The only other sounds were the calls of the gulls and the terns that at times winged over us.

We eventually reached a small quiet inlet and into this Nils guided the boats. On either side of us was an area of rock, bogland, and a mass of bright, colourful dwarf plants, with which the whole region was covered for this short period of summer and autumn. A big patch of fluffy cotton grass made the swampland quite white, and near by amongst thick grasses, the big yellow balls of the globe flower shone out in a dazzling array. This flower, something like a giant closed buttercup, grew to a height of over eighteen inches.

The whole place seemed thick with colour and Anna-Maria sprang delightedly among the flowers, plucking a big bunch, but we knew they would soon wilt and be worthless by the time we reached the camp again. The sight of the arctic flowers is something so welcome. Nature seems to compensate for the long northern winter by a glorious display of colours, both now in early summer and especially in the autumn, when the leaves of the birch trees turn to a mass of burning red and gold.

We were waiting here for the owners of the nets that we saw deep in the crystal-clear water at this point.

They were Norwegian fishermen, whose catches of the very firm coal-fish were heavy in these quiet parts, and were obtained without much trouble.

They soon arrived, quite elderly men, with very wizened and weather-tanned faces, and drew up the nets, disclosing a very large catch of these silver fish. They were some three to four years old, they told me and were fished in these waters from March to December. There was a ready sale for them, as they are excellent eating, whether boiled or fried.

Nils gave them a hand, not with any motive of just being helpful but with the hope that when they had finished he would be able to have a net of fish for himself. And so it proved! One of the men picked up a long pole with a deep net at the end and scooped it full of fish, which he tipped into the bottom of Nils's boat. This was to be our cue to leave, and with a cheerful satisfied grin Nils pulled us out of the small bay and into the open fjord again.

We were now heading the boats towards the small island where the lovely, delicate, silver-swallow arctic terns were breeding. They rose long before we reached them, and flew around us with anxious cries, darting almost down to our heads. We could well understand their fright, for they are little disturbed by humans here, except the occasional Lapp family, who come for their eggs at times.

We climbed up among the rocks, and nests and eggs seemed to be everywhere, with many small and very attractive youngsters dashing into the cover of the stones and thick clumps of grass.

I put up a small tent to act as a hide, and prepared to spend some time waiting for the birds to return to the nests. The others left me alone, to go to a further headland for a time, and there make a fire and cook some of the eggs for a meal for us, with bread and coffee.

I have always been impressed greatly by the arctic tern, because this slim bird carries out an amazing and complicated migration over the globe each year.

In the latter part of August they concentrate on eating as much as possible, to build up a thick layer of fat before their journey. Towards the end of August the high-arctic regions are deserted by them, and the low-arctic areas, such as we were in, they would leave in September.

Starting in small parties of not more than ten or twenty birds, the Canadian and Greenland birds come across the Atlantic south of Iceland, reaching European waters, from as far as southern England, south to Portugal. During this long flight in September they do not rest or feed —they just fly, keeping in an eastern or south-easterly direction, and moving at less than a hundred feet above the sea.

They usually stay there for a short time, to recover their strength after the long flight. But before the end of October they have again all left Europe, and fly onwards to the south, along the west coast of Africa, keeping well out to sea. Some seem to winter in these waters, which are rich in food, but the majority continue again southwards to South African seas.

Even this may not be the end of the journey, however, for they sometimes round the Cape, northward into the Indian Ocean, where they are seen as far away as Madagascar. One that was recovered after being ringed was found to have travelled 11,000 miles in less than three months—surely a feat at which we can marvel.

But some of these remarkable birds, continue even further, flying until they reach *antarctic* regions. There they spend the winter, keeping to the clearings in the pack-ice belt, where they feed on krill, which is very plentiful.

Thus, in crossing the globe almost from pole to pole, the graceful arctic tern undertakes a voyage longer than any other creature in the world, even including the large whales, which are also great travellers. And in its flight it obtains more sunlight than any other living object.

I was now admiring them as they settled all around me, when over my head swooped down one of the main enemies of the terns—the sooty-black arctic skua. With its long pointed tail feathers, it reminded me of a large bat. The skuas are hated by the terns, who rose to the attack immediately and cried intensely until they had passed over them.

Later Anna discovered a fluffy, dark youngster that a pair of skuas had reared at the base of a rock, and I went over to try to film it. This was my mistake, as I was soon to discover, for one thing one must admire about the skuas is their bravery when defending their young.

They both dived at me, missing my head by a fraction of an inch, it seemed, and my hat was soon sent flying. There was an immensely angry 'swiiish' from their wings as they 'braked' at the last second. Time after time they attacked until I was forced to give up photography, being too busy raising my arms to defend myself.

Meanwhile little Anna-Maria was having a fine time, gathering and admiring the small arctic tern chicks, which were the first she had seen, but eventually we left the area of the nests, to allow the birds to settle down, and went over to where the wood fire, made from driftwood from along the shore, was burning and the water boiling.

Anna-Maria climbed over the slippery rocks with the speed and agility of a goat. She was quickly growing to be as much a part of nature, and the nomad life, as her parents; and even Josef was affected by her jolly laughter.

From the boiling water in the old coffee-pot, Anna pulled out some of the terns' eggs, and offered them to me. They were orange in colour and tasty, even if fishy. We had no salt, which was a pity, but with the rough bread and margarine and a cup of coffee to follow, we had a meal that was as good in these surroundings as if it had cost a fortune.

We sat high above the water, on a flat rock, enjoying the sun and the play of light along the wide sweep of the fjord. All was absolutely still. On both sides the mountains were deeply reflected, giving an almost completely double picture and it was difficult to tell which was reality and which was reflection.

Into a dim blue distance we looked, until the haze of the atmosphere enveloped our view. The only sounds came from the terns, which began to settle, and the kittiwakes that also flew around us. The skuas were content now that we had left their youngsters in peace. As the smoke from the twig and driftwood fire rose straight into the very still air the peace of the afternoon was such, in this lonely fjord, that even Anna and Nils were happy to sit and gaze in silence for a long time over the water. I think it was one of the most bewitching moments of my whole stay in the north.

Little Anna–Maria lay down at her mother's feet, curled around and went to sleep. Josef sat silently by my side, whilst I watched the elegant terns land one by one on the rocks and then take their places over the eggs, or call to the youngsters that had hidden. Small fish were brought back to feed these young, which would now grow at a fast rate, in time to make the long flight in the autumn. It seemed incredible that they could be ready in such a short while.

Arctic skuas and Arctic terns . . . both birds that belong entirely to this faraway world, where the summer is short, but warm enough to give them all the food they need, from the fjords, for their young.

In the golden-reddish glow of the evening light we left for the journey back to the camp. As we moved the waves from the prow of the leading boat made the clear reflections of the steep slopes dance and break up in the water. Again we saw small parties of grazing reindeer and occasionally a deer swimming alone far from the shore. They seemed to enjoy swimming, and moved at quite a good speed, with head held high.

The day had been long, and the heady clear air almost intoxicating. It would be easy to sleep this night.

I arrived back at the hut in the evening, carrying several fine coal-fish, and was greeted with great pleasure by the crow, who immediately

began to pick at one of them. He was never far away in the evening, and had spotted us from a long way off. 'Was there ever a more
faithful feathered friend?' I thought, feeling a good deal of tenderness
for this black and grey bird from the wild, who shared my wilderness
home.

I had noticed that Nils had also been getting quite attached to
Charlie, and before many days had passed I discovered they, too, had
found a youngster in one of the nests and had decided to try to tame it
as a family pet. It became rather amusing, because, although they were
successful at this, whenever the poor bird tried to fly over, with Nils,
to my hut it was immediately chased off by Charlie, who attacked it
fiercely. He was having no other crow around his own domain, that
was soon clear.

As I lay on my bed that night, in a sleeping-bag and on my reindeer-
fur mattress, I thought how greatly my education had been widened. I
saw again before me Josef's calm brown eyes, as he showed me his
papers. How much he could write, given the ability, about his life.

CHAPTER 12

Recollections of a Hard Life

OLD Fru Ellen Christine Sara had amazingly good eyesight, despite her advancing years, and could always pick out reindeer on the slopes in the far distance over the fjord water.

She was a stern-faced woman, little given to smiling at me, but she had a preference for my hut, finding it much more comfortable than her own. In this way we gradually became more friendly, although the language was a problem for us, and it was Hannah who had to assist at those times. But as Hannah made such excellent coffee, the older woman was soon drawn out, and ready to talk about her life. Wrapping her shawl more closely about her, for the air was mostly cold, and her bones were not young any more, she would gaze out of the door into the distant hills, and talk to Hannah and nod at me. The clouds had hung, nearly all the summer, in deep grey layers, far below the level of the tops of the mountains which surrounded us. It was rather depressing to wake up day after day to this cheerless view. But when the wind blew and the clouds rolled away, the sight of the blue sky exhilarated us all.

It was a period now when the herders often had to be absent for many days at a time. They would prepare for their journey with a few items of food, bread, margarine and dried meat in a small rucksack, together with the dried sedge grass, essential for their feet. They wore no socks, but merely changed the grass when they had wet or perspiring feet. With their dogs, a stick, binoculars, and also a rifle, for shooting any deer they found with broken legs, they were ready for their patrols that were hard and difficult work in this rocky region. It was surprising how often the deer met with accidents, and also the Lapps faced another trouble—poaching from Norwegians, who were quite ready at times to try to shoot the deer. The flesh found a ready sale, for it is excellent eating.

For the women left behind at the camp there was always much to do. Footwear, especially, wears out year by year, and to make a new pair of winter moccasins, or 'skaller' as they are called, requires the head and two legs of a deer, from which the fur is stripped, and plenty of patience and hard sewing. The autumn 'komag' or stronger footwear also had to be made.

Berit and Fru Sara worked hard and well together. Fru Sara oiled the komag with a thick, messy smelly coating of cod oil, kept from the the previous year, and also prepared the large skins for the making of leggings and other clothing.

She was the only one I saw who was content to sit for hours surrounded by a big pile of newly made komag and a tin of the thick black grease. The younger women tried to avoid the smelly job, which took a long time, and left it if possible to the old lady, who accepted it as she did everything else. I always felt that she had no respect for the opinion of anyone but herself; she seemed more friendly with Hannah than any of the others. They could sit and laugh in their strange language for hours together.

She had very much to remember of a long and hard life. Her children were Nils Aslak, Inga Anna, Christine Ragnhild, Marit Aslak, Aslak Aslaksen, Per Aslaksen, Matis Aslaksen, Karin Aslaksdatter, and Berit Ellen, and one who had died.

The naming of children is a very interesting and important part of Lapp life. There is a host of names for members of the various generations—grandparents, parents, present generation, children and grandchildren. For uncles, aunts, brothers-in-law and sisters-in-law there are also terms denoting age, in relation to father, mother, husband and wife.

There are three grades of cousins, first, second and third, and when a marriage is being considered then there is a good deal of thinking around this question of relationship.

It has been the general rule for very many years that a child should be called after someone who has died, and if the child dies, then the name goes to the next child of the same sex to be born. This ensures that the old names are handed down from generation to generation. It was unfortunate that some of the names were branded as 'heathen' by the missionaries. But the Lapps, after a Christian baptism, would often return to their tents and re-christen the child in their own way, and some of the old names have survived until today.

The Lapps use both first name and surnames, and as with the Sara family, an early first name had gradually become the family name. In Norway and Sweden the custom of suffixing *sen* (son), and *datter* (daughter) to the father or mother's name is much used, and so Fru Sara had an Aslaksen (son of Aslak) and Aslaksdatter (daughter of Aslak) among her children.

A man with the name of Mikkel, if his father were called Matte, would be called Matte-Mikkel, but a grandparent's name can also be added before these two, and even at times a great-grandparent's. In this way several generations figure in the same name of the boy or girl.

Many of the ancient names that we call surnames today originated simply from the use of the father's or mother's name, such as Sara, Bigga, Anti, Turi, Ravna, and others. So we arrive at Aslak-Aslaksen Sara, and Karin Aslaksdatter Sara, which effectively explains the relationship to all.

Recently, Norwegian, Swedish and Finnish place names have also begun to be used as surnames, and also unusual occupations, in much the same way that many of our own surnames originated from trades and professions.

Fru Ellen Christine Sara was proud of her long line of children and their many sons and daughters. After a lunch of boiled fish and potatoes in my hut one day, she traced with a stick on the floor, going back over the years, and Hannah translated for me.

All the old lady's life had been spent moving back and forth along the spring and autumn trails, and the children had been born with the ease that comes to those who live so close to the animals. She was eighteen when she married, her husband being some fifteen years older than herself.

Her first child had been born on the spring trail, and she had cut the cord herself with her knife, and then thrown the afterbirth to the following crows. She had never needed a hospital, but like many other Lapp women her teeth had been much destroyed by the pulling through them year by year of the immensely tough, strong sinews from the legs of the deer, which were made into the threads used for sewing clothing and footwear. Twisted between the fingers and wetted with saliva, the sinews eventually assumed a thin but waterproof and very strong reel of thread, but the enamel of the teeth was very quickly worn by this harsh treatment.

She continued with her story . . . a widow two years before the big evacuation in 1944, she had been one of the big group of women and children who had crossed over to Lille-Korfjord, to escape the Germans.

The men had hidden in the hills with the herds of deer, but the Germans had tried to be friendly, wishing to exchange reindeer meat for other food items.

She recalled with a laugh that one of the games of the small children at that time was the hide-and-seek that had a grimmer meaning than usually associated with that game. 'Germans, come and find us, we are here', had been the cry in those days, when life had been even harder than normal.

After the war they had all been able to resume their old way of life again, and the Norwegian Government had assisted them in every way possible. It was thus that Aslak had been able to obtain his grant for the building of the three small winter huts out on the Finnmark Vidda, from which we had started our great trek. Fru Sara did not now follow the long trail with the reindeer herself, finding it too great a strain, but travelled overland by means of various transport, eventually taking the boat from Alta to reach the summer quarters.

'Come with me,' she would suddenly exclaim, and I would follow in the manner that all her children followed her. It was a habit that one soon acquired.

She worked a good deal on the curing of the skins, and it was remarkable what strength she still retained in her very strong hands.

First all the hair had to be scraped from the skins, after which they were soaked in a tub of water, into which had been placed a large amount of birch bark. After a week of this soaking the excessive smell of the skin had been removed, and it was ready to be further treated. She dragged out each skin and then pulled it hard several times round a post to remove the water. Then stretching it into as good a shape as possible, she hung it over a long line, to dry in the air. After this drying, the skins were ready to be used for the making of trousers and also the soft sides of the komags, or autumn footwear.

I never saw Fru Sara idle for long at a time. She was up extremely early in the morning, always with her thick shawl around her shoulders. The crow had a certain affection for her, which she returned. It would never leave when she sat working with a big pile of the komag before her, sleeves rolled up, and hands black with the thick oil. Inside and out she smeared the footwear, until they were really impregnated with the waterproofing oil. They were then left for several days for this to sink into the skin, after which they were ready to use. Charlie used to amuse himself greatly when she worked at these, dragging as many as possible away from her in an almost human game.

Komag must be one of the most difficult of all things to sew. The soles are usually of cowhide, and extremely hard and tough, and how Berit ever managed to push her needle through them and sew the great many stitches needed to make a strong boot, I never knew. I tried it several times myself, but gave up in despair, for my fingers never seemed strong enough to make more than a few stitches. This is where Berit always amazed me, for she was not a strong-looking woman, and very thin, but she and old Fru Sara certainly showed the others how to work at all times.

I asked Berit one day if she would demonstrate for me all the clothing that was hung in the shed by the edge of the fjord.

This she cheerfully agreed to, and sitting with a big pile around her in the heather, she held up one item after another for inspection and also filming. And how proud she was of them!

The thick white 'besks' or winter cloaks, and the fine brown cloaks, were all decorated with braids. These were followed by pure white skaller, or winter footwear, made from the best skins, to be used only on special occasions. Then Aslak's fine best much-decorated clothing was shown, and his long hat with the points, also with a mass of coloured braids. Big warm mittens, skin trousers, warm sleeping-bags . . . what a mass of work and stitching she had around her, and one had to greatly admire a woman who could produce such fine and warm clothing in her primitive environment.

And last she opened her chest with its large key, and took out all her most-treasured golden and silver ornaments, bands and necklaces. I was most impressed by these, for they are not often seen, being carefully stored away to be brought out only at weddings and other feasts.

There was something very likeable about Berit, and one always knew that she would be in good humour, even when the weather was awful and things appeared difficult and miserable.

Even in the middle of the night, which was the time the fjord boat often came to visit the pier, she was always watching closely to see who came from the boat. The warning siren always produced a rush to the pier, and the Lapps were full of eagerness to scrutinize every fresh face, for gossip was one of the things that made the days pass more pleasantly. They never missed a thing, and she told me she never went to bed until the ship had left the pier, and this was often two or three in the morning. Even I became affected by this urge to go to the pier, for it was our only contact with the outside world, and post, newspapers, and fresh supplies were eagerly looked for. There was always a little procession that followed back to the post-house, where we waited for our letters to be sorted and given to us.

But one day saw Berit coming to my hut with a face that had lost all its humour, and I soon shared her bitter feelings.

It was another grey day, and had been raining. She told me that her own dog, a fine animal only one year old, together with the dog that had become such a good companion to me, and which I had hoped to take back to England, had gone off.

According to the law in these far northern districts, the Lapp dogs are supposed to wear a heavy piece of wood suspended from their necks. This is to prevent them chasing the sheep of the Norwegian farmers, for since the olden days there had always been a deal of friction between the nomads and the farmers over this matter of sheep worrying. The nomads had been forced to agree to have clubs of wood hung from their dogs' necks, thus forcing the animal to walk with lowered head and legs apart.

This, to the mind of most people, is a very cruel custom, for no dog can ever walk or run in any comfort with such an unwieldy load tied to its neck. Often we had discussed it, but there was nothing they could do, for if the dogs were found out without their clubs, then the farmer thought he had a perfect right to shoot them, and could plead sheep-worrying in defence.

The two dogs had gone in search of a bitch from a near-by settle-

24. The glow of the evening sun filling the fjord with golden light is one of the delights of these northern waters.

25. Nils and Anna-Maria Sara watch from their hut for signs of the reindeer on the slopes on the opposite face.

ment, and had been out for many hours. Berit had become anxious and
had gone in pursuit of them herself in the late evening. She had now
returned, with as much rage as I ever saw shown by a Lapp, saying
bitterly that they had both been shot.

I was as much upset and angered as she. A Lapp without his dog is
like a shepherd who has lost his most valuable helper and comrade. We
both knew that the dogs had been tied with their wooden halters when
they went out, but the man who had shot them had defended himself
by alleging they were entirely free, and he could shoot them if he liked.

There was more behind it than that. We knew that the nomads were
not liked by some of the farmers, and this was a welcome opportunity
of hurting them in the most effective way.

It was with some pleasure that during the morning I saw the boat of
the Lensmann (the sheriffs of the north, and the only type of police that
patrolled these regions) approach the pier.

Berit reported to them, bitterly asking them to do something for her,
but she received little sympathy from the two men.

'They can shoot them if they go loose after sheep,' was all the two
men would say. Berit returned to my hut, and her rage was such that
if she had had the farmer near her then she would cheerfully have stuck
her large knife into him . . . so she said and I believed her.

She would not weep over a dog, as it had no soul, so she thought, but
she had lost a valuable unpaid, willing servant, and I had also lost a fine
friend. We were both seething with indignation, and wondering how
we could get this injustice put right.

Berit would be forced to buy another dog to train for the autumn,
and this would cost her many kroners that she could ill afford.

We decided that we would not leave the matter in this unsatisfactory
state, and that I should make an official complaint to the authorities in
Alta. After this we felt a little better. It was at moments like this that the
Lapps felt glad to have me with them, for they knew that my word
would carry some weight.

That same evening we went together in search of the farmer, and a
very angry scene took place between us, especially when I saw the really
lovely dog that I had wished to own so much lying dead for no good
reason. We scared the man considerably before we left, and Berit said
she would lay a curse upon him that he would never forget.

I think he believed her, and began to apologize. We told him it was too late, and that we would have the whole matter settled by the Lens-mann, for Berit wanted compensation for her dog, and I wanted justice for her.

There are times when even the Lapps have to come into contact with a side of life that is very unpleasant to them, and this is why they like to keep as much to themselves as possible.

It was easy to understand, but as we sat together in the late evening, looking over the serene fjord, waiting for the steamer to arrive, we began to relax again, and even to smile a bit, for it is impossible to find a Lapp in bad humour for a long period.

CHAPTER 13

A Work that has No Ending

I N order to please Berit a little, I said I would work more on the hut, making it so fine that her mother might even like to live there the next summer. She was very pleased about this, and to get some materials I went over to the Internat, or boarding-school, that the Government had built on a rather unlikely spot on this big remote island.

It had amazed me, the first time I had rounded the last bend of the fjord and had seen Altneset in the distance. In this wilderness, where the village only consisted of half a dozen wooden houses, or so it seemed, there was a very impressive and finely built school standing by itself and looking quite out of place.

I had asked about it as soon as we arrived, and was told that all the scattered fishermen's children for many miles around came and stayed there during term-time. It cost the Government a considerable sum each year to collect them by boats from the surrounding islands and villages, and the expense of housing, feeding and teaching them was also very high. There were spotless kitchens that would have been suitable for a very fine hotel, and the whole buildings were a revelation to me, so far out here in this arctic region.

The great difficulty was in getting teachers to this isolated spot, but two very smart flats had been provided in the buildings, and I later met the two young married Norwegian couples who were the teaching staff. They were very glad to see an Englishman, and I spent many hours with them. One of the wives had to teach in English, but she was very shy about it, and was glad of the opportunity of speaking with me.

At the moment the school was empty, for it was the long summer holiday, and workmen were repainting some of the rooms. It was to them I turned for assistance for my own work.

A very pleasant and helpful painter greeted me, and cheerfully gave me a supply of white paper and paste, for papering over the ceiling and walls of my hut.

It was no easy job, this paperhanging, for we found that the paper stretched tightly as the hut became infernally hot with the bread baking, then it would suddenly split along one of the cracks. But it certainly made a great difference to the appearance generally, and old Fru Sara was very impressed, and I gained her confidence even more. I also managed to obtain some paint from the school, and decorated a bit, after which the men came over, to admire the work and sample some of our coffee and a little reindeer meat.

My hut soon became the centre for meetings of all the Lapps. They are not used to any embellishments at all in their huts, and certainly no furniture to speak of, and as I had now created for them a very pleasant place, from the wreck that we had at first found, they naturally accepted that I should welcome them at any hour of the day or night.

Sleep was always difficult for me because of the constant and strong light day and night, and to be wakened at about 6 a.m. by someone tapping on the window, and asking for breakfast, was a little disturbing at times. This is exactly what happened, however; for if a Lapp herder, wandering over the fjells in search of his groups of deer, made his way to our family group, he was always directed to my hut. It was impossible to ever be impolite, and hospitality was accepted as the very natural thing. They themselves would always welcome a stranger into their tents or huts, and I had to learn to think and act as they did, which I soon found myself doing, aided by help from some of the women.

I did not see so much of the men at this time, for they were constantly away, and would not take me, saying that I could never keep up with them on such trips. They were probably right, so I remained, almost in charge of the camp, as it were.

There were many occasions now when I had the chance to trail a small family party of deer which had taken a liking to the very rich and thick grass, young willows and small birch trees that were now growing on the rising slopes behind our huts.

The water continued to pour down, for which we were thankful, and its purity was such that to drink it was to taste a more sweet, peaty, crystal clear drink than I had ever experienced. We felt no danger, for it came pouring from the melting snow on the heights, and had been filtered through the peat before it reached us. Nature itself was ensuring that our supply was as clean and fresh as it was possible to ask.

As we had no method of keeping food cold in the hut, we placed it in containers in the water. The weather was certainly never very warm at the best of times, but the hut became so overheated when the old stove was lit that somewhere was needed in the cool, if only for the margarine and such items.

I had had the good fortune to have a supply of tea sent out all the way from London by Twinings tea company, and very glad of this we all were. Soon the Lapps had developed a liking for tea, and asked for this in preference to coffee when we sat talking together. Perhaps I was having far too great a civilizing effect upon them. Well, they were also teaching me more than I had ever learned from my old university city in the art of looking after myself in a primitive way of life, and I was more than thankful to them.

Taking the crow, my stick, and cameras around my neck, and a small rucksack of food and drink, I would often set out for the day from the hut, following a slippery trail by the side of the water, until I reached the heights from which I could see the deer. Here was the favourite spot of a group, that now looked in excellent condition. They did not belong to the Sara family, whose whole herd were just over the water on another part of the island, where we could observe them through binoculars from time to time. These belonged to Anders Mikklesen Sara, a relative from Beckajord, another small outpost along the fjord side, where his little group had their huts.

It was he who came very early one morning and awakened me. We had not met before, but soon felt old friends, as I was now being accepted as almost a part of the big Sara clan. The Scottish clans came to mind the more I knew of the Sara Lapps, for they seemed to extend over wide areas, and embrace many generations of relatives.

Hannah was also a businesswoman, and she now wanted to do a deal with Anders for me. I had a pair of leather riding-boots—very impressive to look at, but completely useless to me in these regions—and I wished to have a fine reindeer skin from him, that was if he could be persuaded to take the boots in exchange. What he would do with them I did not know, but they would in any case be a fine status-symbol in his family.

At any rate, that was Hannah's argument, as they sat outside on the short grass, by the poles of the old tent. This we only used when members of the family sometimes came over to visit us by boat on a Sunday. It was then that we would pull the old cloth round the poles and light a fire in the centre of the tent in the traditional manner. I did not like to see the Lapps discarding their ancient ways for the huts, and I tried to encourage them to use the tent as much as possible. They felt pleased about this, for they seldom met foreigners in this way who were genuinely interested in preserving their cultural life as they had always known it.

Anders complained bitterly about the swarms of mosquitoes that caused such trouble inland. He wished that like us he had his herd close to the coast and water, where we were completely free of these pests, much to my own relief. He had badly scratched his hands on the stones in the fjells, but Hannah soon had them bandaged. He had an affection for her which was plain to see, and had no desire to leave the huts for a while, if he could stay.

It was agreed that I could have the skin, and he eventually set off again up to the fjells, carrying my boots on his back.

Having set out alone from his base many days before, it would now be days before he returned, but so it had always been, and he thought nothing of it. In his reindeer rucksack he had senna-grass for his feet; bread and margarine in a bladder pouch, and a few other odds and ends, and he wanted no more. It was impossible not to compare his wants with my own, and to wish that one could live as simply and as contentedly as he seemed able to do.

Berit, who worked excessively at the making of the skaller these days, together with Hannah, liked to relate to me more stories of the olden days, when the tent life was lived summer and winter, and huts were not thought of.

In her mother's youth, all the clothing in winter was sewed by the poor light cast by the fire, and the women were expected to take their turn at the lonely and cold task of watching over the deer. They had to rear the children, chop the wood from the forests of thin birch trees, maintain a supply of food on which they could exist, and all with the barest of materials.

But the tent floors were always covered thickly with fine twigs of birch, with reindeer skins covering them, and they can be warmer and more hygienic places than a poor hut. This has also been proved true in many of the Eskimo villages, where they have deserted altogether their ancient ways.

Today the Lapps do not have the same fight against the elements as they had previously. They even have old-age pensions, sick benefit, and a good child allowance from the Government, which makes a tremendous difference to their feeling of security. They have much to thank the Norwegian Government for in this respect, but as the number of Lapps living in the far north of Norway is greater by far than in any other country, they have probably had more consideration by Government planners because of this.

It was a fascinating experience watching Berit preparing to make a pair of skaller, exactly as they have been made for hundreds of years.

There she sat with an old sailcloth over her knees, surrounded by a pile of reindeer legs, and several heads.

It was quite a bloody sight, but she ignored this, and with a very expert handling of the knife, cut round the head so that the whole of the skin could be drawn off in one piece. This would form the sole of the skaller, and immediately the heads were thrown aside the crow was after them, picking at the eyes, which he considered a great feast.

From the legs the skin was also stripped with speed and skill, and when she had a pile gathered, she took them all to the side of the hut, where she pulled them into a flat shape and nailed them to the wooden wall. There they would all be left for several days, to be cured by the sun and the weather, in the rough manner that the Lapps have always known.

After the curing, they were taken down, and the exact pattern of the feet and the sides of the skaller cut out for pair after pair. It is not for fun or decoration that the Lapp footwear has a rather comical-looking curved point at the end of each foot. These were originally for hooking under the leather bands on the skis, which could then hold them fast.

It was difficult and tiring work, sewing the skins. They had to be well made, and as strong as possible, for they must last all winter, and take the thick padding of senna-grass as well as the feet inside. The

Lapps depend entirely on these skaller for winter wear, and there are certainly no better boots for a dry snow climate. They are very light in weight, very warm, and excellent in every way. They are quite useless in the wet, however, when they must be discarded for thicker boots, and these days the men usually set off in rubber boots over the fjells, finding them the best.

Another job that was very tiring was the scraping of the big skins, in preparation for their soaking in water. The tool used had a wooden handle, with a curved blade of iron and was held in both hands. It took a long time to remove all the hair from a skin, but a well-made pair of leggings will last several years, for the leather is tough, pliable and hard-wearing.

When Aslak, Nils or Josef set off across the fjord in their small boat for the heights opposite to us, where the deer roamed among the peaks, they were never without their lassoes, which were as important a part of their equipment as the stick and the dog.

They are really a legacy from the days of the wild-reindeer trapping, but in the great round-up of the autumn I was to see them in action day after day, and expertly they have to be thrown.

These days the lasso is usually made of hemp rope, bought ready made, and with a horn or metal ring at one end to make the slip-noose. Formerly it had to be made by hand, using leather, sinews and root fibres. The sinew lasso is immensely strong, and this was the one probably used by the old Lapps when hunting the wild deer.

The blouse-like jackets that they always wear, of blue cloth, were now becoming very worn. They were very useful when they wished to carry any extra loads, as the wide low belts supported anything they liked to stuff inside. A mass of decorations covered the belts, for the Lapp likes to decorate everything he owns, even to the knife handles and sheaths.

The Lapp knife is a most versatile piece of equipment, and what he or she would do without it I have no idea. It serves for almost any tool, and as a knife and fork at meal-times. The knives the Sara family had were long and straight, with wooden handles, but others were sometimes of bone, which were decorated with the most beautifully carved patterns. The sheath can also be patterned in this way, and to see a skilful piece of bone or leather pattern carving is to realize the Lapps have a sense of design that is quite remarkable.

The men took with them as usual several fish hooks, for fish played a great part in their diet when they were away for several days. Hannah and Berit saw that they had a good supply of bread, and they always carried dried reindeer meat, which is nourishing, even though extremely tough to chew.

We never knew, as they set out, when they would again appear. There would be no way of communicating with them, although later I found that Ole Gaino had a walkie-talkie outfit, with which he and old Per Kemi could keep in contact over the fjells. I have no idea where they had obtained the money for this, but they were as proud as a couple of children over this piece of equipment, and liked to use it as often as possible, just for the pleasure of hearing the voice from a long distance coming so close. This extra help was indeed welcome, especially to a family group that had not many men herders, and must work even harder because of this.

The bad summer weather we were having, continued all through July, during which month we saw the sun on only about three days. This was not only unpleasant but dangerous to the herders, for the cloud came down so low that it formed a thick mist along the whole of the slopes. The rocks became very wet and slippery and the men could easily lose contact with each other, and the deer fall into the crevices.

On every occasion they went the three men returned with a dead reindeer, so that we now had a constant supply of meat; but there was little pleasure about this, as the loss of each deer meant a good deal to the family financially.

CHAPTER 14

Fishermen—Crofters—Builders

ONE never ceases to be amazed at the way the Norwegian fisher-men have managed to cultivate every possible patch of earth in this far northern region. There is certainly not much of it, and what there is is usually filled with rocks that have to be removed before a tiny field can be planted with potatoes, which is the only vegetable that I found growing in a cultivated state here.

I mention this because although the Lapps have no possibility of growing greenfoods or potatoes for themselves the fishermen who form these small isolated villages all try to grow what they can. They also gather in as much hay from the long and rich grass that grows very fast under the continual twenty-four-hour summer daylight.

I had made friends with one typical old seaman, Hansen, who spoke a deal of English which he had picked up on his voyages to America. He was over fifty, tough and friendly, and his wife, typical of these northern wive, was able to weave the most wonderful patterns into colourful woollen pullovers and gloves. She also managed the small 'farm' they contrived to run, to add to the income from fishing.

This is quite the normal procedure, the combination of fisherman-crofter. The Hansens kept a few sheep, chickens, and one could see a cow or two also in the fields.

One day he invited me over by boat to his house at Komagfjord, because on the morrow he intended to start cutting the hay, and I wanted to be there. It was the 30th of July and a clear and bright even-ing when I arrived.

Next morning before breakfast, which is usually eaten at the time that we would eat lunch, and is a healthy meal with much milk-drinking, hard breads, butter and a mass of various items for spreading on the bread, we commenced the hay-cutting.

It is impossible to describe what a setting of beauty Hansen had behind him as he swung his scythe. The grass was filled so thickly with yellow flowers resembling our buttercup that it seemed like a yellow field instead of green.

The fjord was absolutely still. Every detail of the slopes, and the boats along the shore, was reflected in the water, and when the sun rose ever higher, then indeed one could understand the love of these hardy people for this life, which can be so peaceful and calm one day, and have such raging storms the next.

I helped with the raking of the hay, which, after it was cut, was hung for several days on long lines of wire to dry. This always seemed a more efficient way to dry hay than letting it lie in the fields, as I had always seen in England; for the wind can blow through it freely, and it loses little of its richness in such drying.

Hansen told me that he needed some 2,500 kilos of hay for each cow from October to May, when they had to be permanently kept indoors, and this would cost about £50 if he had to buy it. As he also had to provide the cow with meal, there was not much profit if it gave him about £100 worth of milk per year.

Therefore they had to try to cut every yard of hay possible, and he was thankful that it seemed in such good condition this year. When one thinks that these fields had been deep under snow only a week or two previously, and now were filled with a really rich and long grass, one realizes the power of the arctic sun and the continual daylight.

If one has never visited these northern parts, it is almost impossible to imagine the fast growth of plant and tree. One day everything is still deep winter, or so it seems on the surface to the untrained eye, and then, overnight, the whole of the countryside appears in a green haze of new leaves, and as soon as the snow leaves the slopes and the fields, then a rash of small and larger flowers of the most brilliant colours burst forth. They have been waiting, under the snow, to be free from their covering, which has kept them warm and protected them from the biting winds.

The sudden arrival of the spring in the far north is a most moving experience, and both the Lapps and the crofter-fishermen commented on it many times to me. I was deeply impressed by it, as many travellers in the past have been.

In the evening, when we were still at work on the small fields, that sloped downwards towards the shore and the rocks, the local steamer came round the bend of the fjord. It was heading for Komagfjord, and as it passed the Hansen house the skipper gave a blast on the siren, which echoed far and clear in this stillness. If ever there was a sight of quiet peace it was at that moment, with the hay hung, fresh smelling, on the wires, the snow still on the mountain-tops behind it, and the fjord steamer slowly moving past. This was the face of the north that many never see—only those whose lives are spent there. It is a face that only shows for such a short period, for the greater part of each year deep snow covers all, and the cold is severe. Chickens, cows and sheep are all kept indoors, needing a good deal more attention than if they were free to roam, and feeding has to be plentiful to keep them warm.

Hansen and his wife had carefully cleared a very stony patch for the growing of potatoes, which have to be of a type that are ready to harvest in about eight weeks. They have no time for a long growth, and are often very small. But when one thinks that everything has to be brought by boat to these villages, then every kilo of hay and every sack of potatoes becomes even more valuable.

These people were typical of many fishermen's families, but Hansen now said he was tired of the life. Months of separation from his wife and son each year no longer pleased him, and he was putting a broom at the mast of his boat—the traditional way of announcing it was for sale.

He had decided to give up and go in for chicken rearing, he told me. Whether it was a good idea I did not know, but he was full of enthusiasm himself. Fishing can be a hard, cold and chancy business, for after the owner of the boat has taken from each catch the amount for two and a half men (for himself and the boat) the rest of the money is divided equally between the crew. There is a firm market these days, of course, in great contrast to the olden days when the fishermen were at the mercy of speculators, who waited for their boats and bought up their catches at the cheapest possible price.

A near-by wooden house by the side of the fjord, with land and a cowshed, had just been sold to a young fisherman and his wife, for the low sum of £600. This certainly seemed a bargain to me, as the house was sound, even if in the full blast of the wind, and I have no doubt they will weather many a storm there and raise a family of small boys who will carry on the tradition of the north.

Nothing seems to dampen the spirits of these people, and there were even times when I wished that some of them would find something to complain about. If one moaned about the weather, then they merely laughed, and the troubles of the rest of the world hardly concerned them. I found from these months of living far removed from our normal civilization that one's mind becomes detached to a great extent from the stress to which the businessmen and the diplomats of the world's capitals are subjected, and problems are seen perhaps in a clearer and more balanced perspective.

The potatoes had been laid along the ditches dragged over Hansen's small and stony field in late June, and he was hoping to raise some 1,000 kilo from this patch. It seemed a great deal to me, for they had to mature at a fast rate, but he was always an optimist.

The old spinning-wheel is not so often used by the wives these days, but Mrs Hansen spent many hours at hers.

After the sheep were sheared the wool was sent to a factory to be properly cleaned from the dirt and grease. Then it was pulled over a board with many wires, forming a brush that combed it into some sort of order. It was then ready to be spun into lengths of wool on the wheel, and fascinating it was to watch this ancient process.

The Norwegians, as well as the Lapps, are very attracted by bright colours, perhaps as a compensation for the long, dark winters, and the pullovers that Mrs Hansen made were a mass of really lovely patterns.

I found this, too, at the local school, which I was invited to visit on their 'open' day, when the pupils displayed their skill with wood-work or with weaving. These boys and girls were certainly clever, and one was forced back to the realization that civilization has destroyed much of the desire and even the ability to create and make things for oneself, as these people had to do.

Just as the Lapps made all their own articles as far as was possible, so the Norwegian fishermen in this region also were skilful at building their own, excellently insulated, wooden houses. This was a most important part of life in the far north here. After the Germans had burnt all the houses in their retreat along the coast during the Second World War, the returning Norwegians simply had to become builders, even if they had no experience. A house has to be well built, to withstand the cold of the winter, but even Hansen had built his own, much to my admiration. He could have obtained the services of one or two men from the district who were builders, but the cost always had to be kept as low as possible, and it was necessary therefore, to do as much work as possible oneself.

The Government were of great help in providing a long-term loan at very low rates of interest, and there was the choice of several plans that the local office would send to a prospective fisherman-builder.

At the very end of the string of houses that formed the small village of Komagfjord was the family of Axel Ring. I went there to hear of his plans, for this was a perfect example of what had to be done when a new house was to be built.

He had been one of many who had returned after the war to find nothing but a burnt-out wreck standing on his ground, and had been forced to build as best he could for his family.

He had lived in this house, which was now very shabby, since then, with his wife and four children who shared his hard life as a fisherman. But now he wanted to have a modern home, as did all the others.

We sat down together and discussed the whole project, and he got out the plans. The house would cost some £3,000, but he would only have to find about £500, for the State would advance him the rest and give him very many years to pay back. The plans had been purchased for about £5 from the local State Architect, but the actual work was left for Ring himself to arrange.

The site he had chosen was just about as close to the edge of the water as possible, and I imagine that in every storm spray would dash against his windows. I asked him if he did not feel it would be better to move it a little further back, but he laughed and said they wanted to be as near as possible.

This fascination with the life seemed to affect the people to an extent that was quite unbelievable, but I grew to accept it, and during the months ahead I returned from Altneset at times to watch the progress of this house, which actually stood almost on the spot where in autumn we would bring over the reindeer, to start their long trek back to the Vidda.

It was fascinating to watch the building grow. Ring had to transport all the wood out himself, the steamer having brought it from Alta to as far as the pier at Komagfjord. Pile after pile of planks and timber for the framework were fetched by Ring in his small motor-driven boat, and two men from a nearby village were employed by him to erect the framework. The three worked with a will, and soon the house began to assume its simple shape. It would be thickly insulated with many layers of materials that had been found most suitable for this climate, and although he was no expert at building, I found that by the autumn, they had together nearly all the comforts of modern life, with electricity, good bathroom and modern kitchen equipment.

There is something to greatly admire about men who still must fetch their wood and build their houses in this way. But without the sound and valuable Government help it would be impossible. Many times I was left wondering how the Norwegian State obtained enough capital to finance all this building. Taxes are certainly high, and it seemed as if they needed to be, for the population of Norway is very small. The country has an enormously long and thin land area, which makes all communication difficult, and therefore more costly.

On my way back from Rings, I met a group of the men who were carrying the electricity over these difficult and mountainous regions. I was invited to watch their work, and saw them boring holes in the immensely hard granite to a depth of some one and a half metres, in order to blast with dynamite holes into which the poles could be fixed. Each pole has to be really firmly placed to stand the climatic conditions here. Day after day, in the still air, the sounds of this blasting could be heard for several miles, as gradually the lines were being extended.

These were tough men, and some of the most likeable I ever met. One, Ragnar Knutsen, a most powerful man, became a visitor to my hut when he was in the district, bringing me empty dynamite boxes, as he thought they would make good shelving. He was right, of course, and they also made good seats.

The men used strong climbing-irons on their feet for fixing the wires to the tops of the poles, and they could be away from home for long periods on this work, especially when the weather was bad. But it was a life that they became used to, and did not seem to want to change. They were a cheerful gang at all times.

I returned to Altneset with the fjord steamer, taking back with me a fine piece of salmon, for which I had paid Ring only about five shillings. It would have cost many times that much in any shop.

26. The low cloud lifts to show the mountains on the other side of the fjord. The mountains were often invisible in the mists.

27. The reindeer herd swimming the fjord on the first stage of their return migration in the middle of October.

Life was being reduced to its most simple complex, and even a haircut, which I now badly needed, was no problem, as one of the wives in the village was glad to offer her untrained services, whilst we talked about all the matters that interested her in the England I had left.

Both the Lapps and the crow greeted me loudly. Hannah had been baking, and her skill with the very broken old stove, which I understood had been found by the Lapps abandoned on the shore somewhere, was something of a marvel.

The pile of reindeer heads from which Berit had stripped the skin, had been hacked with her knife into smaller pieces, for cooking, for nothing would be wasted, and the brains were considered a great delicacy. They were mixed with meal, and made into an excellent cake, and the tongue was also eaten with relish.

As I watched them all at work, it began to seem as if I had been part of this world all my life. My riding-breeches were now dirty, and my thick dark green pullover, filled with holes. My face was a deep brown, and I even carried my own Lapp knife at all times, ready to use in the same manner as they did. The feeling of wanting to be a part of this way of life, and the thought that one day, not far off, I would leave them, filled me with a sadness that hung heavily upon me. I had only been away for a short period, but it was as if I had returned to my own family, and they were now accepting me so much that Berit seriously began to talk of me taking some deer and starting up reindeer herding with them. If my physical strength had been greater it would have been a great temptation, but one has to be born to such a life, I felt, and I knew that I could never run over the rocks in the same way that Aslak and Josef did in pursuit of the animals.

CHAPTER 15

Old Songs and Marriage Customs

STRONG winds continued to blow along the fjord during the first days of August, and at times it felt very much like autumn.

It was decided that Berit and Hannah were to return to the winter settlement at Gasgoletten in the heart of the Vidda, to prepare to attend a wedding, and they were to be away some time.

When the day came, Andersson took them by boat to Alta, from which town they could travel inland by bus. It would be quite unlike the long overland journey we had made in the spring.

With them away, the men out in the mountains on the island after their deer, and old Fru Sara also absent for a time with another family along the coast, I was left alone with the camp and the crow.

It felt a desolate place at that moment. It was now the middle of August, with a hard, very cold wind blowing, but with a bright sun. At times I wondered what it would now be like on the crowded holiday beaches back home in England. The contrast could hardly have been greater.

This was a lonely outpost life. It seemed I had the fjord to myself, and the cries of the crows and the gulls were the only sound until the steamer appeared, often late at night.

Suddenly one day Nils returned. I heard his boat engine far over the water, and I was certainly glad to see him. He came over to the hut with some reindeer meat, and was really an excellent cook, when his wife ever gave him the chance to show his skill. He soon had the most delicious steaks fried.

This was also a fine chance for him to talk and please himself for a time, and he asked me if I would like to make some home-brewed beer. This idea intrigued me. The ingredients were quite simple to obtain, and he thought the hut would be very suitable for its fermenting period.

We should need 2 kilos of sugar, 1 kilo malt, 2 hektos of yeast, 1 glass of molasses, and 18 litres of water.

This mixture had to stand for three days in a warm place, with the scum being taken from the top at intervals, and then placed in a cold room for one day, after which it was ready for drinking.

It sounded simple enough, and I managed to obtain the ingredients from the local shop. With much enthusiasm Nils mixed everything together in a large container he had procured from the the back of his own hut, and we set it all in a corner of my hut, which was quite warm, contemplating it with much smacking of lips as the fermentation began He was going to enjoy my hut, I could see that, when the women were away.

The days passed and the ale was ready. It was a very pleasant drink, and quite strong. We had many glasses with the reindeer meat and fish that he brought to the hut, and then I had a visit from his wife, Anna, who was becoming curious about his long absences during the day-time. He did not neglect his fishing, however, and we fished together in the fjord for cod and coal-fish for the whole of the family.

A small rough track led along a winding trail towards the next village of Hakstabben. It was the most perfect setting for a Western film that ever could be imagined. On one side were towering and jagged rocks, over which the raven flew, and on the other the rocks dropped steeply down to the water. Unpaved, and as little used as a road could be, it had taken, nevertheless, several years to build, and one wondered why anyone had taken the trouble. All the winter and for the greater part of the year, in fact, it was under snow, and as there were no vehicles of any sort in the area, it did not seem worth the effort. If the people from one village wanted to visit another, they mostly went by boat, either their own, or with the fjord steamer.

Along this track were strung out, with a good distance between each, small wooden farmhouses. In the fields of each the hay was hanging, which seemed rather late, but it was in such good quantity this season that the farmers all appeared to be quite pleased.

To call at one of these crofts was to receive a very hearty welcome.

Immediately the coffee-pot was put on the stove, and the table set with various cakes and biscuits, all home-baked, and open sandwiches.

It was impossible to escape from the house without long conversations. Their interest in life in England was very great, and their feeling of friendship for me as an Englishman moving. I wondered often whether there was any other country where I should have been received with such warmth, mostly because of my nationality.

I related as much as I could about life as I knew and had lived it, and then looked through masses of old photos, which were always produced with the family albums. At times I felt, on such a visit, like a priest must have felt making a big parish round of visits. Naturally they were pleased to see a stranger and talk. Their lives were so isolated in the shadow of these towering rocks, which would soon be deep under snow again, and yet there was not one who wished to ever leave this life.

Sometimes I climbed high over crags, where the hooded crows had nests in small trees bent by the wind, and where the ravens nested year after year. The farmhouses looked like toys below, with the lines of hay swung heavily between the sagging poles.

This was a life that could be, in the heart of a bitterly cold and dark winter, as isolated as is possible to imagine, and even on a day in mid-August I returned to my hut in the early evening with fingers that were so cold that I could hardly make a cup of tea.

It was now beginning to be darker, and a lamp would soon be necessary. This I managed to borrow from the little post-house, so that we could have at least a yellow glow shining along the fjord from the small hut window in the late evenings.

At times in the still of the twilight I would stand, with my stick over my shoulder and the crow seated silently upon it, feeling very much like a modern Robinson Crusoe. I felt I had the world to myself, for my hut stood quite alone with an uninterrupted view along this majestic fjord.

Then I would return to the warmth inside, and make a meal of boiled potatoes and fish, or reindeer meat. Charlie would sit on his stick in the corner, waiting for his share, and watching me, often with head turned on one side, looking deep in thought. The bird was also becoming very much a part of this life, which must heve seemed as strange for him as it did for me. Although perfectly free, he had no desire to return to his own kind, but had developed a dependence upon me from which I could not escape.

It was a welcome morning when Hannah and Berit returned. The loneliness without them had been rather a strain, for Nils and Anna and even Josef had also been away again on a trip with the herd. Little Anna-Maria had been left alone with Ellen while the family were away, for the goats must be milked, and they seemed to manage well enough together.

The women were full of stories about the swarms of midges on the plain and they had been very glad to move away as quickly as possible. We were fortunate here at the coast to be free of them.

We took this occasion to have a family reunion group, sitting round the fire in the open by the tent. The young boys were very expert at fishing from the boats that Nils and Aslak owned, and they would make as large a catch as possible when relatives were coming over; so that we now had a pile of fish before us to cook over the fire, on sticks, in the heat of the embers. They tasted quite delicious done this way. Old Fru Sara became as animated as a young girl with her family around her; for several of them had come from neighbouring villages in their small boats for this Sunday gathering.

It was a moving experience to be a part of one of these get-togethers, where Fru Sara was so much obeyed, even if another relative was there who was also the head of a growing family. There was much talking and laughing, drinking of their strong coffee, and discussion about the state of the reindeer groups.

Everything centred round the deer, of course, and gossip was exchanged about the number that had been lost by each group during the time they had been at the coast. The numbers of calves born was also of the greatest interest to each member of the family.

Some herds had had their calving-grounds on the actual spring migration trip, whilst others were born at the summer grounds. The does do not like disturbance when they are calving, but it is an interesting experience to watch the behaviour of the calf soon after it is born. Often it is dropped on to the snow, where it lies for a while, steaming with its body warmth. The doe licks it all over carefully, and after about an hour it is up on its thin legs, which hardly seem strong enough to support its light weight, but having had a little milk it is ready to totter along behind its mother.

Calf-marking on the ears begins in some places as early as July, but the Sara family would wait until the big autumn round-up. Every deer has to be marked, as this is the only way of identification.

After a deal of discussion and coffee-drinking, one or other of the men started to sing in the strange and remarkable manner that is so peculiar to the Lapps. They are not really a musical people, and their way of singing is known as *juoigos*, or 'joiking' as they always called it. It is a form of story telling, often quite improvised, most often sung in a high-pitched voice, to the theme of such sounds, 'Valla-valla, lu-lu-lu, nana-nana' and others, after which a verse is sung. The melody rises and falls, and can continue until it induces a kind of sleepy detachment. When heard in the darkness, around a Lapp fire, it was a most eerie and primitive sound, and it does, in fact, have an affinity with some of the North Asiatic folk music.

On and on the singing went and then suddenly, as with the Scottish bagpipes, it comes to a halt without warning. The verses can be inspired by almost anything that happens in the Lapp life—the glaciers that we passed on the way to the coast—a herd of reindeer on the move—a beautiful girl a person one wishes to honour or even curse. It can be of joy or sorrow.

There are lyrics about the ancient Gods and other spirits, and the melody often depicts the flight of a bird, the waves on the shore, or the wide sweep of the mountains. The music will soar up when the singer tells of a tall mountain peak, and Nils, who seemed to have a very sensitive mind, was easily the most accomplished singer of these strange and often moving verses that I met in my travels.

The songs are mostly composed by the singers themselves, but some can be learned and passed down from generation to generation, and Nils seemed to have learned in this way more than any of the others. Old Fru Sara sat and nodded her head in approval, while the others tried to join in when they felt they knew the words a little, and then I must say the whole group sounded very unmusical.

It is interesting to note that some 1,500 old songs, collected with a great deal of trouble, from among the Finnish and the Norwegian Lapps, have been published and at the Tromsø Museum there is a collection of tape-recordings of this ancient folk music. Nils had also shown me how he could make a flute, which is one of the only instruments the Lapps play. He used a hollow angelica stem and cut about five holes along this, and a mouth-hole at the end where the stem made a fork. He blew into this, and produced a range of notes that were quite attractive as long as the stem was fairly fresh. It was not often used today, he told me, and perhaps it is because the old *juoigos* have always given the Lapps such good opportunities for expressing their feelings, that they have not invented more musical instruments.

The very closeness with nature that is possibly some of the most dramatic and stimulating in the world because of its amazing contrasts, from winter darkness and cold, to eternal summer light and beauty, has meant that the Lapps have much poetry in their temperament, even though they have never been great writers.

The oldest examples that we know of Lapp folk-poetry are two ancient *juoigos* lyrics, recorded by the Lapp priest, Olaf Sirma in Torne. These were published by Schefferus in 1673 in his famed *Lapponia*. The themes of these lyrics have travelled through the literature of the world, and such poets as Herder, Longfellow, Runeberg, Franzen, and Kleist have interpreted them. They can be recognized in Swedish literature in Runeberg's 'Journey to the Beloved' and in Franzen's 'Run, my good Reindeer'.

As I sat listening to Nils singing I thought how easily the old *noaides* must have been able to sing themselves into a trance, with the aid of their drums. But I was reminded of another side of Lapp life that is not so pleasant. In common with other primitive peoples, spirit has now become a part of their life, when they can afford to buy the bottles of strong Bränvinn. To see a group of Lapps trying to sing when they have drunk a good deal of this stuff is a rather pitiful sight. I also found it depressing to see them, in a town, sitting round a café juke-box. They were completely out of place, and looked lost and forlorn.

As I write this, there is much discussion in the newspapers of the north about the way that spirit consumption has sprung to a record height in Greenland. The Eskimos are now able to purchase it, and there it is considered something of a 'status-symbol' to be able to drink as much, and more, than the Danish workmen who are building big blocks of flats by the coast. I feel that the Eskimoes have lost much from their contacts with civilization, and this could easily happen to the Lapps if it were not for the fact that usually they are too busy to make trips into the small towns. Also they are usually very short of money until they sell the slaughtered deer in the autumn. Then they can be forgiven if they take a boat into Hammerfest and bring back a supply of strong clear spirit, for they have earned it after their months of hard work.

I was to see them drink, but never became unpleasant, and I must say that the old Sara family have retained their ancient customs, habits and independence in a manner that is truly remarkable, and is to be greatly admired. Only strong family discipline can maintain such a tradition, and the contrast between the manner in which the boys and girls obeyed their parents without question and the behaviour of the Swedish youngsters I have seen in the Stockholm area is immense.

One of my Swedish woman acquaintances told me that she had taken her sixteen-year-old daughter to the doctor for her supply of P-pills. Of course it was necessary, she replied, when I asked her if she had to do this. It was better than her coming home with a baby, as some of her friends had done at the same age.

It has become so accepted, this earlier and earlier sex-life, and it was a pleasure to see that the Lapp family had no such problem. The girls appeared to be very moral and correct, and I cannot think of a Lapp mother who would take it for granted that her daughter would begin to want a sex life as soon as it was humanly possible.

The word divorce is something that has little meaning to a Lapp. Once they are married, then they remain so, and the large families that I found among them were firmly united. The children were some of the jolliest, and certainly the healthiest, I have ever seen, and when I think of the sturdy independence of little five-year-old Anna-Maria, and of how she will grow to continue the tradition of her so ancient family, then I have little fear that the Lapp culture as I know it will not survive for many years.

I remember Aslak saying to me, early in our friendship, that in Oslo the people 'Think we have horns and a long tail between our legs'! This was said laughingly, of course, but it is amazing how little really is known in the cities, even in Scandinavia, of the life and habits of these people who are so worthy of study. To live with them as I did was to soon become infected with the sorrow or joy that the elements themselves can induce a person to feel. It was so easy to understand that the small baby, who was now carried in the Komsa all summer, and who still looked up at the trees and the heavens with wide eyes, would be strongly influenced all her life by her early years on the trail. She would go to school, to a modern school, where she would be taught many useful things that could fit her for another way of life, but her loyalty to the family would almost certainly draw her back to the old life. She would be able to speak good Norwegian, and feel herself a part of the Norwegian race, but she would not want to turn from her own people, who are proud of belonging to this small but ancient Lapp culture.

Josef was a very good example, and as his father sat singing by the light of the fire on these family gatherings he would watch Nils with his brown eyes and often smile at me. He enjoyed the life so much that it never occurred to him to want to change, even though he knew much more about the outer world than did his father.

There would be plenty of quite attractive girls from among whom he could later choose a wife, and I noticed that already he was thinking about them in many ways.

Marriages were often discussed when we sat round the fire, and I asked as much about their old customs as I could. I knew very well the importance and the feasting that is attached to a Lapp wedding, and although things change with the years, a Lapp ceremony is still something worth travelling many miles to see, even if only for its beauty of clothing.

It was the usual custom, among the Finnmark Lapps, for a young man to try to pull one of the mittens from a girl's hands if he had serious thoughts about her. If she did not prevent him, it indicated that he was welcomed by her.

As with most peoples, the young men carried gifts to their girls— silk scarves, rings and brooches, but these were returned if nothing came of the association.

There was an old procedure, still kept up in many families, for 'asking for the hand' of the young lady. The young man had to come either with a group, or at least one man or woman who would act as his 'courting-man' or 'courting-woman'. This custom has much similarity to that of some of the old Indian tribes, and it is necessary for the man or woman to be able to talk well, to meet any objections that might arise from the girl's parents.

In some places guns were let off to show the group was approaching, and if it was winter, then the reindeer of the courtship sledge had to try to drive right to the tent or house without attracting too much attention from the family dogs. This was no easy matter, for the dogs make a furious noise at the approach of any stranger, as I found on many occasions.

The two youngsters had to appear to be quite unconcerned whilst the parents and the spokesman talked about a large number of matters that had nothing to do with the marriage.

It was some time before the actual subject of the wedding was discussed. But after it was settled, with the number of deer that would be exchanged forming often an important part in the talks, then the atmosphere would be more relaxed, and Lapp hospitality could show itself freely.

In some parts the negotiations were even more complicated. The courting-sledge must drive three times round the tent or house, and if the girl herself came out to unharness the reindeer of the young man, then he could be sure of a welcome. He had little chance if she did not, however. It was the spokesman who would ask if they might make some coffee when they entered, and if permission was granted, he would serve this to the parents of the bride. If they accepted this with good friendship, then the discussions would start.

The young suitor had to produce presents for the parents, and it was considered right for the brothers of the young girl to rather ridicule the presents, and also probably the young man. For this, the spokesman must have suitable replies. A lot depended often upon this courting-assistant, but as I so well know the Lapps and their sense of humour, I can well imagine that most of the ritual was carried out in a spirit of good humour if the young man was at all liked in the family.

It was the usual custom for the bride to bring a dowry to the marriage settlement. It could be reindeer, or perhaps a boat and fishing-tackle, for the coast Lapps. The Lapps who were permanently settled, perhaps inland as small farmers, might give a piece of their land.

From early times it was the usual custom for the young man to join forces with the family of the bride, but the couple had their own tent as quickly as possible. An extra man as a herdsman was always very welcome, and as he would also bring his own deer, then the herd would be increased, and the family widened as soon as the couple had children.

There have to be sufficient men to cover all the watches for the reindeer herd, and therefore a large group together is better than a lone family. For this purpose the Sara group, consisting of the three families

I had met out on the Vidda, had a better chance of controlling the herds in winter on their vast desert of snow.

If the Lapps were forced to take servants, either a man as herder, or a girl as a cook and also a herder, then they would be given a certain number of reindeer each year and also clothing. This I found still to be the custom, but money also now enters into the agreement. A servant is always a part of the family, eating in the same way, and he or she can easily become a son-in-law or a daughter-in-law. There have been many examples of a careful young man saving his deer until he had enough to start up on his own with a wife.

Children are warmly welcomed by the Lapps, and Nils used to shake his head sadly when he saw me in my hut. 'You will never get a family like this,' he would exclaim with a wry smile, and then went on to describe the delights of the large sleeping-bag he and his wife shared. Despite his large family, his eyes would light up with pleasure when he spoke of such things, and he regarded me rather sadly. I must confess that I often felt the same way when I was in the heart of a family group, for they always seemed happy, always having enough to do to keep them well occupied.

CHAPTER 16

The Lonely Heights of Vinna Island

AUGUST was passing quickly, and with it the short summer. It had been dry, despite the bad clouds, but our water supply had not dried up, even though it had been reduced to a mere trickle down the sides of the rocks.

We always had to keep an anxious eye upon this, as we had no other supply for our drinking.

Further along the coast of Seiland, to the north, was another island known as Vinna, which was the summer grazing-land for Per Kemi and his group. This island, although quite small, was an ideal spot, and certainly one of the most attractive that could be imagined.

One day Hannah and I decided to pay them a visit, for there would be excellent opportunities for filming the deer on the heights on the island, from all the accounts I had heard.

The day we were to travel proved very warm. We hastily packed some things, and had a lunch of boiled potatoes and coal-fish. Hannah varied the fish cooking so that one day it was fried and another boiled. Fish had to form our main food, together with potatoes, for the reindeer meat was kept for special occasions.

We set out in Andersson's *Kristine*, but before we could start I had to have a considerable argument with him because he refused absolutely to take my crow as a passenger. Charlie listened to all our somewhat heated conversation, perched on my shoulder. Andersson was as superstitious as most seamen, and thought the bird would bring bad luck to the boat. I was almost ready to say I would not go, but eventually decided to leave my good friend behind with Fru Sara, who was very fond of him. As we set off, I saw Charlie struggling in her hands, desperate to follow.

I could understand how useful Andersson was to the family with his fishing-boat, and Berit knew what she was doing in encouraging his courtship; but Fru Sara continued to receive him coolly, for she had no desire whatever for Berit to marry outside the Lapp race. There was nothing wrong with him as a good Norwegian, but he was not a Lapp, and even when he promised to build a fine solid house, and provide her with her own room, the old lady looked at him impassively and without any real friendship.

Andersson often came and complained to me about his treatment. He liked a stiff drink, and usually felt like having one after a session with Fru Sara. He was a man with a good heart under a rough exterior, and I knew that his intentions were the best for them all. He was determined to build his house, and hope for the best, and I think he spent more time than he could afford coming over from the mainland in his boat as often as possible.

The little wizened Fru Kemi, Per's wife, looking like a gnome beside Andersson, had been on a visit to our group. Now Berit, she, Hannah and myself were all to visit Vinna for a time.

This was not the finish of the contingent that commenced the journey, however, for Josef, Nils and Anna also started with us. Anna travelled in Nil's boat, filled with rucksacks and equipment, which we pulled behind us on a long line.

They were to leave us as soon as the very primitive crude hut which they would make their headquarters for a few days, whilst they climbed up the extremely steep sides to round up some deer, was sighted.

At first the trip commenced in fine form, with the bright sun making the fjord look very pleasant and cheerful. The whole group were lively and talkative and Andersson was also in good humour, for he could now have Berit with him in his control cabin, and from time to time they would peer down at the rest of us, sheltering from the wind beneath. The Lapps always made all their trips seem like summer excursions, but when one thought of what lay ahead for Nils, Anna and Josef, cut off as they would be on the heights for days, then one quickly realized it was not all a picnic and there might be real hardship ahead for them.

Soon the wind grew colder, and I wished I had on much warmer clothes. The fjells were very steep here and majestic, and one could imagine the immense pressures of the ice during the time when they had been pressed and twisted by the weight of the Ice Age fields.

It was very easy to visualize the intense coldness of this region in the winter, and soon we had a taste of it ourselves, when a heavy mist began to close in upon us, blocking out the welcome warmth of the sun and making it impossible for us to see more than a few yards ahead. Dampness was everywhere, and we all became much quieter.

But it was along this now inhospitable coast that we were to set free Nils's boat, and soon he and Anna began to row away from us, and were quickly swallowed up into the mist. They did not seem unduly disturbed, but gave us a cheerful wave as they disappeared.

Our journey continued, with the engine of the fishing-boat muffled as we edged slowly along the fjord. Andersson had to keep a very sharp look-out now, for it was not easy for him in these narrow waters.

Eventually we reached a little inlet, and a small boat was lowered from our side, into which Berit and young Josef clambered. Berit was to tow Josef over, and he would eventually join up with his parents.

Just ahead of us, in the water, a very fine buck reindeer suddenly appeared, swimming with head high, and antlers red where he had been rubbing the 'velvet' loose. It was now hanging in strips, but before we could reach him, he had scrambled out of the water, shaken himself hard and was up and away into the mist at a fast pace.

The deer wandered over a wide area here, and it was quite difficult to see how the herders ever controlled them. They managed it, however, in their own peculiar manner, knowing where to look, of course, and Josef seemed quite happy to be left on his own in such surroundings where a normal fifteen-year-old boy would have felt completely lost.

We continued further, and gradually the mist cleared as we neared the island of Vinna. It was now early evening, and the sun again broke through, bathing the small island in light.

There seemed no sign of life, and the few small houses had all long been deserted, except for the summer hut of the Kemi family. It was rather an eerie sensation as we landed in the dead quietness at the end of a small pier, where once had been life. All had left the island, however, for living had been too difficult here all the year round.

Per Kemi's hut stood by the side of the still water. It was teeming with coal-fish, and in the 'harbour' was a huge, tank-like enclosure, in which they were stored for a time by the local fishermen.

I had never before seen this procedure, and it was one of the reasons why the Kemi family were attached to this spot, despite its utter desolation and lack of any neighbours whatever.

When we reached the hut there was a note pinned to the door saying the whole family were out after the reindeer, which they must round up for swimming the short distance back to the main island of Seiland, after which they would travel overland until they reached the coast opposite the mainland. There the deer would swim for about half and hour, landing at a fairly level spot from which they could make their way to the traditional rutting area.

We waited for a while, and Hannah began, as was usual with her, to bake fresh bread for all of us. Until I lived with the Lapps I had never realized just how much bread a family can eat, and how often it has to be baked.

She continued with this task for some hours, and during this time the Kemi family returned, very damp and rather annoyed with the thick mist, which had prevented them finding many of their deer.

The sleeping arrangements here were as primitive as elsewhere, with the whole family curling up on the floor round the walls of the main room, and pulling blankets over themselves as usual. In my honour, however, they had prepared a 'bed' in another very small room. This consisted of three fish boxes, on which reindeer skins had been laid. It was no better than the floor as far as I could see, but I thanked them profusely for their trouble, and tried to sleep, for it was now very late. Never did I find the Lapps in any hurry to sleep, and yet they were very early risers.

It rained during the night, and the first sight of the morning was gloomy in the extreme, with another heavy mist hanging along the fjord, shutting out any long view.

Mikkel, the son of Per Kemi who was now serving with the Norwegian Army for his compulsory training, had returned home to help his father with the rounding up of the deer. He was one of those who was being made very discontented with the old life. His new contacts had

28. (*Opposite*) After their summer grazing the reindeer are in excellent condition as they descend from the heights. The herd starts to collect at the round-up area in September.

29. Hannah and Per Kemi hold the head while Karin Gaino tries her hand at milking a deer; nowadays the deer are rarely milked—goats' milk being used instead.

30. Per Kemi with his own reindeer at the autumn round-up site.

opened up avenues of thought that he would never have had but for this training, and I soon found he had no real desire to return to reindeer herding, even though little Per Kemi was now far past the time when he should have been springing, like a deer himself, over the rocks.

As soon as we had eaten a wind sprang up, clearing the mist, and the sun made a very welcome appearance.

The men now felt in better spirits, and even Mikkel smiled a little. But they had no desire to take me with them. They were a most secretive family, and Ole Gaino, who was connected to them by marriage, could only apologize in his smiling way, looking at me keenly with his blue eyes before they departed at a fast rate.

I knew the reason. They did not want me, as an outsider, to see the size of their herd. Neither did they want me to slow their progress over this difficult and dangerous terrain. This was quite normal, and I did not resent it, but decided, whilst the women worked and cooked, to do the stupid thing, and go off to climb the heights on my own.

One should never do this in normal circumstances, for a slip can be fatal, and a companion a life-saver, but I had no choice, as so often happened on this long expedition.

Loaded down with my cameras, tripod, and a couple of sandwiches and a flask of coffee for my lunch, I left the hut, which was on some flat stones by the edge of the fjord, and started to climb the very slippery, wet rocks, which rose steeply massed to a great height, behind. They were covered with vegetation and the rains had made finding footholds a very slow and tricky operation. As my cameras swung violently away from me, at each upward movement, it was all I could do to keep my balance. I was only too aware of the danger of falling backwards to the hard granite rock surface below.

Reaching the first level plateau after much effort, I stopped for breath, and to admire the wonderful vista that lay before me over the water. Ranges of small rocky islands jutted from the clear water, becoming more and more blue as they receded into the misty distance. The sun was glittering on the water now, but the wind was blowing hard up here, and struck my face coldly.

This was an area of loose stones underfoot. From the reindeer droppings and the way the stunted willows and birches had been nibbled, it was possible to trace the path of at least some of the deer. Reindeer eat very lightly, taking a leaf here and another there, and often they roam over a very wide area in search of food. Only their droppings, and in the swampy fields, the deep imprints of their feet, show at times where they have been.

I pressed on, reaching another flat plain that spread out into the distance, thickly covered with lush grass. An inland lake surrounded by a fringe of tall stiff green reeds lay ahead of me; it was a rather surprising sight, but it was obviously a favourite haunt of the deer, and I could see against the skyline the silhouette of a fine buck, with head turned towards me.

It was a good distance away, and I had to cross a swampy field and then climb a slippery slope to reach it, but I hoped it would lead me to a group.

I then came close to a bad accident. Half-way up the slope, my foot slipped, and I began to slide down among a shower of loose rocks. I reached out desperately and clutched a small birch tree, gashing my left hand badly in doing so. The small tree held me, luckily, but my camera and tripod continued to slide. I managed to hold on, and then very slowly and carefully, edged down until I could rescue the equipment, which had lodged against a tree.

I rested in the valley again, and tied up my hands. The camera did not appear to be damaged, which was something of a miracle. But I realized I had been near to the kind of accident that makes lone travel in these hills so dangerous, and why I had been advised against it.

I was thinking this, and wondering just which way to climb, when I heard a clanking sound from a bell like that which a draught reindeer always has around its neck. The sound carries a long distance, and then I saw two figures, the Lapp with the animal behind him, like toys high up the slope among the thick vegetation.

Above them, on the top of the hills, there then appeared several other deer, standing out like silent black figures silhouetted against the light.

The deer began to descend the slope, having heard the bell, and I remained hidden behind a large rock, waiting for their approach. It was a fine opportunity for filming them in such lonely and wild surroundings, where they appeared so different to the big herd that had moved over the white plain in spring.

Here they resembled again their wild ancestors, and they became indeed much harder to approach during the summer. Their coats were now thick, and a rich grey-brown in colour, although many of the youngsters were white. They were all in excellent condition because of the good feeding and the fact that on these heights they were not worried by the midges. It was a very good summer area, and I felt the Kemi family were fortunate to have this site. Certainly Aslak Sara would have liked it.

The family group passed silently quite close to me, not being aware of my presence, as I remained quite still by the rock. It was a sight that few people see, reindeer in such surroundings, quite free to roam where they will in a setting that had some of the appearance of the Scottish Highlands, only with more jagged slopes.

As I stood thus I was surprised by a light sound behind me, and as if he had sprung out of the ground, Per Kemi appeared by my side. If ever there was a Lapp who looked the nomad he was, it was this man. Thin and small, his clothes as worn and patched as any I ever saw, and his puck-like face, surmounted by the mop of greyish hair, he seemed to move as lightly as any deer over the rocks, and I had no idea that he had been anywhere near me.

We sat for a short while together. He asked me if I had any food, and I shared my two sandwiches with him. He took one eagerly and half of my coffee, then, as suddenly as he had appeared, he silently left me again. There was no word, only a sudden disappearance, and the next I saw of him was moving at great speed high up the slope.

Well, my food supply was gone! The day was only half over, and it was no use going back now, so I began to climb the rocks again.

It was some time before I reached the top, and when I did so there was no sign of Peri Kemi, the other Lapp or of any deer; it was as if I was utterly alone on these heights, and the grandeur of the scene was overwhelming. Far to the north I could even see Hammerfest. The only sound was the moan of the wind, and the cries of a pair of ravens that flew over me.

I sat, sheltering from the cold by the side of a rock and looked around. I then saw I was not alone, for looking down at me was the finest specimen of a reindeer that any herd could possess . . . it was, in fact, the leader, who remained aloof in this manner for long periods.

We looked at each other from a long range, and I was filled with the longing to film him. But I felt that any move from me might immediately make him leave, so I remained quite still.

Much to my complete surprise, the fine buck began to descend the rocks, coming towards me. Nearer and nearer it came, showing the magnificent antlers that it carried so lightly, although they are of considerable weight.

It passed behind me, on the other side of the large rock. This was the last I thought would be seen of it, but I was wrong. The deer emerged, only a few yards from me, but standing on a path beneath me, overlooking the water that now lay so far below us.

He turned and looked at me with his large soft eyes, and I noticed the thick velvet that was as yet untouched on his antlers, and his very fine brown coat.

So we remained . . . the two of us sheltering from the wind. It was a moment of time I shall never forget. The sun made the sea sparkle, and a small fishing-boat passing the island seemed like a very small toy. The deer was standing on the edge of the path, gazing down at the boat, and behind it the lines of rocky islets rising from the sea disappeared into a misty blueness.

Whether the deer was glad of my company I do not know, but I thought with envy of the pride of owning such a fine animal.

Neither of us moved, and an hour passed. Not a wasted hour, however, but one of complete surrender to the beauty of such a scene.

I looked at my watch. It was five in the afternoon. It was better to leave. I felt very thirsty, having had so little to drink all day, also the herders might well feel I was the cause of them missing their leading reindeer, just when they were rounding the groups up into a herd again.

Carefully I began to descend, and the deer followed me down the very steep path. Being loaded down with cameras that were heavy and that swung away from the body all the time, and with one hand always holding a tripod, my progress was very slow.

With care I reached the level ground again, with the big reindeer still keeping silently quite close to me. I felt rather proud of this. It would be something to boast about to the Lapps! I always felt very inferior to them as they moved so easily over the rocks. Now perhaps I could feel a little elated to think that this fine animal had attached itself to me in this way.

Climbing up towards me suddenly appeared the forms of Hannah and Fru Kemi. They had come in search of me, having become worried by this time, and Fru Kemi was indeed glad to see the deer behind me. She took control of it, and disappeared alone, with it trailing behind her.

In her thin high voice she talked to it, and it responded to her. She was on her way to join the family group at the spot where they would assemble the herd to swim the short distance in the evening light. Where exactly this spot was Hannah and I did not know. They were keeping it from my knowledge for the good reason that they had no desire for me to film them. They had none of the openness of the Sara group, but had retained much of the suspicion of strangers that the nomads have always maintained.

Back at the hut at last, I was more than glad of a good rest and a hot meal. But it was many hours before the family group returned; they had certainly worked very hard.

It was nearly two in the morning when I heard them eventually settle on the floor. What amazing resistance they had to all normal discomforts, or was it just that I was an example of how civilized life has softened the great majority of us? I envied them. My knowledge of many subjects was far superior to theirs, but at the same time a feeling of inferiority was easy to acquire when living in the wild in this way, for which the vast majority of us are now so unfitted.

What pitiful possessions they had, and yet how little they asked from life. Their health was good, and their food came mostly from the natural things around them. They had little need for other human contacts, and as far as I ever saw, no Lapp ever appeared to have any of the complexes that bring so many patients to our modern hospitals. They were self-reliant, unafraid of anything, and accepted their way of life in a spirit of good humour. I found that as long as I was ready to laugh at myself, at my own mistakes, falls, and other awkward habits, then all was well. They could accept me, and laugh with me.

The men had seen me with the big deer, and had been rather impressed. They talked about it a lot the next day. It was the first time, Per Kemi told me, that he had known such a thing happen in this way, and it pushed up my ego quite a bit. They seemed to treat me with a little more respect and less suspicion after this episode. I had shown that I was not afraid to venture alone in the heights, and this was what they admired. Any fool, they thought, could stand about watching them; but they could only give their friendship to a stranger who would try to stand on his own feet, even if he was no expert.

One of them had even witnessed my fall down the rocks, for although they had treated me with such seeming indifference, they had been keeping a watch on me of which I had been quite unaware. If I had been in danger from my fall, then it would not have been long before one of the herders would have been with me. It was because of this that Per Kemi had so suddenly appeared at my side, he afterwards confided in me.

This was a side of the Lapp nature that I had not seen before, for the Sara family, with all their friendliness, never seemed to take any personal notice of me. It was this feeling of inadequate personal contact that I felt at times, for my knowledge of Swedish, which was all I had with which to communicate with them, was understood in part, but I am sure not in its whole context, and without Hannah's assistance I would not have learned so much about them as I had.

I appeared to be taken into the heart of this group more from that day, and it was a pleasant and warming feeling.

This lonely island, although devoid of humans other than the summer nomad family, was not without its wild life, which was quite unmolested here. Goats, for instance, moved among the fjell rocks. They were kept for their milk, and also for the cheese that was made when their milk supply was at its highest.

When I was watching them the next day, sitting quite quiet, a stoat popped out of a hole between the rocks fairly close to me. It stood on its hind legs, front paws held as high as possible in an attitude of listening. Then, as suddenly as it came, it dashed back into another hole.

That evening the men returned, one of them carrying over his shoulders a young deer they had found with a dislocated joint. This they had shot, and then cut up the body and parcelled it neatly into the skin. The meat was welcomed, but the men were annoyed at having still to search for several stray deer that had slipped through their round-up. They could not afford to lose any, and before they left the island they had to make sure that none remained. It was a task that I did not envy them.

The Lapps have found the value of insurance, and they now pay in some 25 kroner each year to a fund for the purchase of fencing for the summer and autumn round-up area, also perhaps a summer hut, or even the loss of too many deer from the herd of one family. This fund, together with provisions made by the State for sick benefit, child allowances, etc., has removed some of the worry from the economics of the nomads.

CHAPTER 17

A Period of Restlessness

IT was the evening of the 28th August . . . a Saturday. At 10.30 that evening Hannah and I were to leave Per Kemi and the island of Vinna, and accompany Ole Gaino and another Lapp herder in his boat along the fjord to Eivageide, where their deer would assemble for the autumn round-up. I so vividly remembered leaving them with all their belongings piled on the end of the same pier, after the swimming over of their reindeer to the shore close by, in May.

It seemed a long time since that evening, when the 'pram' behind the fishing-boat had been filled with the deer. And yet the time had passed so quickly. It was now almost autumn, and the short summer nearly over.

The trip in the boat, with the outboard motor, was made at a good speed, making the cold of the night air bite even deeper into the face. On either side of us the slopes rose blackly. Behind us, the setting sun made a brilliant spectacle, but it was dark before we arrived at Ole Gaino's hut.

His wife was asleep on the floor, surrounded by several children, but she quickly roused herself, and made us warming coffee, which we needed at that hour.

My own bed was as primitive as theirs that night, and I was thankful to pull a couple of grubby-looking blankets over me and curl with as good an imitation of their own position as I could manage.

Sunday dawned bright, windless and warm. Both men, Ole Gaino and Per Sara, a brother of Aslak, were soon away again in their boat, but the womenfolk dressed themselves and the children in their finest clothing for me to photograph them all in the afternoon in the near-by heather. They were a colourful and fine sight. I was always impressed by the way they managed to keep themselves and the children in such good condition.

This was a good chance for the youngsters to show me some of their games. The boys were very proud of their skill at the old game of rein-deer hunting. They took it in turns to hold the antlers in front of their heads, twisting and running to avoid being caught by the lassos of the other boys. It was good fun, and also very useful for their training.

The girls were much quieter. They mostly contented themselves with bringing out the small bone weaving-frames they carried in their chests, and showing me how they could make lengths of coloured braids. They had not lost their skill with this old art, and as I mentioned earlier, the Lapps, especially the nomads of this area, are very fond of a great many decorative braids and bands around their headwear and costumes.

They were a very merry group that peaceful Sunday afternoon. It passed without any further work, and I felt it was good for them also to have an excuse to dress up a little and relax. It is not very often that they did so, and even now they were constantly on the look-out for deer.

Fru Gaino had saved the life of one of the calves born on the spring trail and rejected by the doe. She had weaned it on milk from a bottle, and now it followed her like a dog. Every little while it came pushing and nudging at her, and springing on its hind legs after the milk in the glass bottle. It would make an ideal draught animal, she explained, being so tame and used to humans.

I mention this because that same evening Ole returned and loaned me his 'cottage-type' Norwegian tent, in which I could remain during my stay there. This I set up on level ground close to their huts, and placed several reindeer skins over the floor to make a warm covering. As I sat in the tent in the fading light of the still evening, the reindeer calf suddenly appeared in the tent opening, and then came right inside. It was a most appealing animal and took food readily from me.

After about a week I felt I wanted to return to Altneset, to see that the crow was all right. Also it was not wise to leave my belongings for too long, as my hut only had a poor lock that could be easily forced.

Again it was very late, about 1.30 in the morning, when the small steamer arrived at the pier, and when I reached the hut after the climb up the rocks, I was very glad to make a fire in the stove to warm the hut a little and make cocoa to drink. It felt like home now, this primitive little lonely hut, and the crow was delighted to see me again.

He was asleep on his perch, outside the hut, when I returned, but immediately woke and croaked with much pleasure. He hopped on to my table and rubbed his head against my face, which was a favourite habit.

The next day, bright and sunny, Charlie refused to leave me. Even when I went over for water, he flew low beside me and then perched at the end of the pipe we had fixed into the waterfall. There he drank from the small flow that came from the pipe, whilst I filled our pails.

Already the first of the silver birch trees were beginning to turn yellow. There was a smell of autumn in this remarkable clear and clean air, and there was also a feeling of heaviness in my heart. All too soon the fall of the year would be here and the great adventure would come to an end.

Aslak returned during the day from another look at his deer. He was not at all pleased with the number they had lost during the summer, and he recounted stories to me of how eagles had taken away some of the young calves.

I had seen no eagles in the area myself, but I had to accept his story. Once again he said how much he would like to find a flatter area, and with this I could heartedly agree. The life is hard enough without the perilous rocky slopes on Seiland adding to the burden of the herders.

I took the boat back to Ole Gaino and his family at Eidvageid in the afternoon, and was glad, on arrival, of the meal of fried reindeer steak and potatoes that the family had saved for me. Hannah as usual had not been idle, and twelve long loaves of bread stood on the table in the hut. This bread was a pleasant and tasty part of our diet; it was brown in colour and rough in texture, and far removed from the white bread that is so normal in England.

Josef Josefsen Sara Gaino, one of the sons of Ole, came to sit in the tent and began to discuss the markings that are cut into the ears of the deer to denote ownership. He made a drawing of his own marks in my notebook, signing this carefully underneath. Every Lapp child is very proud when he or she is given a mark of their own, which they will keep all their lives. It is necessary for the youngster to be sixteen before a new marking can be bought and registered, and this costs some 10 kroner or one shilling.

They must become very proficient at cutting the ears with their set of markings, and they assured me that the animals do not suffer when it is done, although it is not wise to do it when the cold is intense, as this can cause frostbite in the cuts.

Ole Gaino wandered into the tent and sitting beside his son and myself looked at the drawings in my notebook.

He loved his life he explained, and would not change it. He felt he had almost a 'tourist' life compared with those whose working hours were controlled by the clock. It was a very interesting statement to hear from a man whose life we think of as a very hard and sometimes bitter struggle.

But as one sat in this tranquil spot and thought of the human ants that move in their crushed masses along the London Underground, for example, every morning and evening of the week, one could well understand his philosophy. We had a small radio, and often listened to the troubles of the world, for that is what the News seemed always to consist of.

'I can work when I want and sleep when I want,' said Ole, 'and in the winter I only have to go and look after the deer.'

I had to smile rather wryly to myself at this remark, for we should hardly think his life was that simple, but when a child is born into it and sees the changing seasons from babyhood on the trail, then no other life seems possible. The spring and autumn migrations are taken in the spirit of a holiday. These men were able to shed whatever worries they had in flights to the heights in the same way as the animals, and after having sampled some of these delights for myself, I could well understand the old poetic songs that had been written in praise of Nature itself.

If these thoughts appear to be somewhat romanticized, then I must plead that I am merely quoting exactly what he and the other Lapps said to me, for they had no feeling of envy towards any other way of life in their thinking.

Ole condemned, as did the others, the State school system for the Lapp children, which spread over some nine years. Although the Government had the best possible motives, and allowed the children to remain with their parents during the summer wanderings, the older Lapps thought that a great deal of interest in the old ways could be lost during this long schooling, which in the case of the boys, was followed by sixteen months of military training when they reached the age of nineteen.

The parents shook their heads at the thought of the ancient arts being learned in schools, as they maintained that the trails must be learned from actual experience, as was everything else connected with their culture. Reindeer herding and breeding must be accepted by the children as their way of life. I could well understand their attitude and also the motives of the Government, but what I saw of the youngsters led me to think that there really is little fear of these nomads losing their skills and identity. The bond of family is so strong, and the interest found in most of the youngsters still so deep, that I feel the Lapps will continue as they have done, with modern aids creeping in at times to make life a little easier.

Mikkel Kemi, the son who was in the middle of his military training, but who had been released to help his father for the important season, joined our group in the tent, and the discussion widened.

He took my notebook, and drew a set of ears for me, showing the marking of father, mother, daughter Ellen Marit Kemi, and his own reindeer. They formed complicated patterns in both ears, and I wondered to myself how they really could be so sure of cutting these exact marks from the ears of an animal that had to be well held down by several people when the job was performed.

September dawned, bright and quite warm. It was the season for the cutting of the vital *senna grass*, a sedge-like thick grass that grows in very swampy land, and is so important for the warmth of the feet during the winter. It reminded me very much of the sedge grass that I had seen being cut at the Nature Reserve at Wicken Fen, near Cambridge, but that sedge had been used for thatching and not for the feet!

The grass is very strong, pliable and over a foot in length. The whole family of women and children gathered in the patch that they had found, and began the cutting with some very rough and quite primitive short curved knives.

The grass does not grow in every area and some families have to travel long distances to do their cutting.

We had the good fortune to have sedge growing very close to the camp, which was a great help, as much of it is necessary to last a family from one year to another.

Even little Berit Anna, who was only seven, was quite good at the cutting, and soon the women and girls were all bent at the serious task of getting as close to the roots as possible. The grass was then placed into big heaps, which were afterwards taken back to the camp.

The women and girls later sat down over a board through which had been driven many long nails. The idea was that each should take a bunch of the grass and vigorously beat it over the nails until it gradually became very soft and the strips very thin.

Bunch after bunch was tied and then hung in a long line in the sun and air, as it must be a very dry hay before it is packed. We were fortunate with the weather, and soon the grass had turned a golden brown, smelling sweet and excellent for the interior of the winter skaller footwear.

I was watching Karin Gaino, wife of Ole, as she worked; she was the typical solid and yet good-humoured Lapp wife. She was much stronger-looking than Ole, who was very thin, with high cheekbones that seemed to protrude almost through his skin.

Karin always showed the most friendly feelings towards me, and seriously suggested that I should start up with them, living as a nomad. I could begin with about forty does and ten ox reindeer, she said! An intriguing thought, but not really a practical one, as far as I could see. Even the cost of buying this small number of deer would be quite high, and I was not really equipped to stand the life, although perhaps with their friendly help I might have succeeded. Twenty years earlier it would have been a challenge, but I felt that it was a little too late, much to my sorrow. I took it as a fine compliment, however, as it cannot be often that a foreigner is offered the chance to become part of a nomadic Lapp group. What a life it could have been . . . it was wonderful to sit and let one's thoughts dwell upon the entirety of it in the beauty of the early September evening.

Once again there was a very fine view along the fjord. The hills now rich in the warm colourings of the grasses, plants and heather, rose steeply on either side until they receded into a hazy distance. It was a time when one could feel in the air a sense of restlessness. Each day now autumn was beginning to impress itself more upon the scene. There is

Mikkel Persen Kemi (son)

Per Mikkelsen Kemi (father)

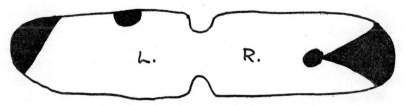

Marit Sara Kemi (mother)

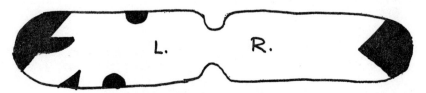

Ellen Marit Kemi (daughter)

REINDEER OWNERSHIP
EAR MARKINGS

After the drawing in the author's notebook,
made by Mikkel Kemi

nothing perhaps so beautiful in nature as this short, glorious season in these far northern regions.

In the bird and animal world, too, physical changes were taking place. Pelts and feathers were becoming thicker, and layers of protective fat were forming to enable each creature to withstand the long freezing winter ahead. The great majority of birds would now be leaving on their migrations, and vast anonymous quietness would descend everywhere when the deep snows came.

Around us now was an area of swamp, with thick clumps of grass poking up out of it. Here we searched for some of the most tasty and sought-after berries of the north . . . the golden cloud berries (rubus chamaemorus). They are called *multebaer* in these parts and are easily the most delicious and valuable of the Arctic berries. Hannah and I looked for them with great eagerness; they glowed like big red and gold balls among the clumps of grass, and we considered ourselves fortunate, for they are never very plentiful. Soon we had collected quite a bagful, and they would be made into rich jam.

In Arctic Canada and Alaska the eskimos also eat these berries, but serve them in a mixture of seal oil and chewed caribou tallow, which has been beaten to the thickness of whipped cream. This treat they call 'Eskimo ice-cream'. The Lapps, however, preferred to preserve them for winter use.

We were to gather many more of these health-giving berries before the autumn snows began, but now we had to travel back to the hut at Altneset, where we would make jam and also cook the reindeer heart that I had obtained from Mikkel for a late dinner.

CHAPTER 18

Thrill of the Autumn Round-up

IT seemed that the autumn weather was going to be better than the whole of the summer.

The hut smelled strongly of the jam that was being made. I had some of it, still warm, with a lunch of steaked reindeer heart. It was Sunday, the 5th of September, and the world felt indeed good.

We had returned to the Altneset hut because at the rear, where the rocks rose steeply out of the swampland, there were an abundance of berries that we must now gather.

The finest and largest bilberries (*Vaccinium ugliginsum*) that I ever saw covered the damp ground, and the sides of the slopes. Only a fraction of the vast mass of berries that this region provides so richly each year are gathered and utilized by bird, beast or human. They grow in their millions.

We gathered large supplies of this fine blue fruit which is delicious when made into a blueberry pie. Ah! the memory of blueberry pie lingers in the thoughts as I write.

The black crowberries (*Empetrum nigrum*) we left alone. Although they are also found everywhere in this region, to our taste they are very bitter and unappealing, and the Lapps did not touch them. Strangely enough, however, the Greenland Eskimos find them a delicacy, and they form a regular and important part of their diet. These berries stand the cold winter very well, and even remain in the same state after being thickly covered with snow.

Another berry that we all well liked was the red cranberry (*Vaccinium vitis-idaea*), which are better known to the Scandinavians as lingon. They are mostly used for jams and jellies, and taste very well with reindeer meat. They are restricted to the southern part of the low-arctic regions, and are always picked in large numbers.

Crowberries, bilberries and the fruits of the juniper are those most eagerly eaten by the animals and the birds. The pellets of the gulls stained the rocks with splashes of blue or red. Even the foxes would eat them, as did the bright-coloured wheatears that had flown round us all the summer.

It was a busy time for us now, as we had to gather as much as possible of what nature provided in the way of food. For winter would soon be here and it was now plainly noticeable how the rich autumn colours were creeping even to the leaves of the berries. The bright undergrowth was thick, and among the grasses grew many edible mushrooms for which the reindeer searched with great pleasure. We also found them very pleasant when we fried them. But strangely enough the Norwegians were afraid to touch them, thinking them poisonous.

It was for us the time of year when the food supply was at its best, and with fish, meat, berries and also mushrooms, we were able to serve meals that were a delight to the palate.

The skies were now beginning to glow yellow-red earlier in the evening and the darkness came sooner. The silver birch trees shone forth in the most glorious blaze of bright yellow and pure gold. As they rustled in the breeze, the whole valley became alive with the sheer beauty of autumn that can never be seen in a more southern region. What a land of contrasts! And how sad that this season of such beauty would only last for a short few days, to be swept away by the first storms of wind, rain and snow.

We had much to do. The time of the summer was now over, and there was again a feeling of excitement in the air, as we knew that the autumn round-up of the deer at Eidvageid was very close at hand, and we all had to be there. Again there was a rush around of packing, and this time we had more to carry.

31. (*Opposite*) It is late October, and the herd has swum back over the fjord. Fru Ellen Sara and her eldest son Nils, who have witnessed this annual scene together for more than half a century, watch over the deer as they assemble in readiness to start the autumn trek back to the winter grounds.

32. Autumn brings millions of vitamin-rich berries, amongst which the blueberries are the most prolific.

33. On a calm day in mid-October, Aslak, Nils and the other herders brought the reindeer over from Seiland; the reindeer are swimming ashore to the mainland.

All was ready, and we set off. But the wind began to blow hard as our boat journeyed along the fjord round the island, and we were glad when we reached the small pier with the high mountain looming at the back. What a fine setting for the drama that was soon to be played out here.

Back at the tent I fussed around by the light of a candle, making everything as comfortable as possible for a windy night. The tent began to shake, but thankfully the strong wind passed, and the next morning was bright, clear and quite still.

So the weather changes almost from hour to hour in these areas, and the clouds that have rolled up then pass away, bringing thick mist followed by strong sun; and all in a very short time.

Suddenly I saw a small group of deer that had appeared on the horizon, looking dark against the light. I was determined to use every opportunity from now on to track and photograph the animals as they began to assemble.

Making my way quietly over the rocks, I scouted round, making a detour, so that at last I came behind and above where I had seen the deer. On the top of the plateau were sixteen fine beasts, quietly nibbling at the grass, they were moving all the time, as is their custom. Behind was the inland lake that was so welcome to the animals. It was a fine sight to see them deep in the water among the reeds, with the calves that followed them which were now quite large.

The velvet hung in ribbons from the antlers of the deer, where they had rubbed it on the rocks, and the antlers themselves were stained red with blood. They looked rather a gory sight, but this would soon pass.

They looked up as I cautiously approached them, but were not unduly disturbed, and watching them I thought of the old days and how different it was when the wild reindeer had to be trapped.

This trapping was immensely hard work, but was conducted in several ways. Perhaps the best method had been the system of lead-in fences that were placed along the known paths of the animals and led to a system of pitfalls. Such pits were to be found all over the Lapp forest areas.

Another old method was to use a few decoy tame deer as a bait for the wild reindeer bucks. Lines of wooden or even rock fences were also built, very wide at the entrance, and gradually becoming narrower until they led into an enclosure. The deer could be driven in this if the Lapps were able to control them enough to lead them into the lane between the fencing.

In Finnmark the keeping of domesticated herds steadily increased during the seventeenth century, and both the coast Lapps and the forest Lapps developed their breeding and evolved their form of nomadism. So we may assume that the nomads that we find today have derived from a simultaneous development in the hunting and fishing cultures of the inland and coast Lapps.

The old Lapps also caught great numbers of grouse, when the flocks reached a great size during the migration season. These were caught in snares set up among the thick scrub and bushes. Animals, such as the fox, otter, ermine, squirrel and even beaver were also caught in large numbers and sold at the fairs.

In the Finnmark region the last wild reindeer were reported shot in 1891 in the Kautokeino area, but as late as 1916 around Alta.

The nomads of today do not have the time, the inclination, or indeed are able to find the wild birds and animals that once roamed so freely. At times they will shoot a fox, and in this region they can have really thick and very lovely pelts of reddish fur, but on the whole they concentrate on merely controlling their herds and seeing that as few calves and deer as possible are lost each year. The days of the wolf packs are also over, and now there are few physical dangers for the deer to face in this way. However, a very severe winter can make the moss very difficult to obtain from under the snow, and then they become very thin, as I had seen when I first saw the herd.

There was now a great air of expectancy in the camp. It was ideally sited, having a good view all round, with the heights rising on all sides in the distance. We sat, it seemed, in a shallow bowl, with the fjord water behind us.

For many years the large flat space at the bottom of these hills had been the spot on which the herd assembled at this time of the year. But a good deal of work had to be done by the whole family before this date, for a fence had to be erected around the whole area, to prevent the herd milling away into the distance again as soon as the lassoing started.

A rotating herd of reindeer can break down a fence very easily, so the wire had to be fixed strongly on to poles firmly set into the ground. The Lapps also used the terrain to help them, for on one side the slopes rose steeply enough to make it unnecessary for any fence to be built.

It was a spot that could not have been better chosen, and was even close to the small pier, so that the buyers, who would come out in fishing-boats to purchase the killed deer, had only a short distance to come to inspect them.

For the Lapps this was perhaps the most important moment of the year, for now they could take into their hands money for the sale of the slaughtered deer, the skins, and antlers, for no part of this animal is wasted whatever.

They had warned me that on this day, which had dawned very bright and promised to be warm and sunny, the deer would arrive.

The men had been out into the hills in search of them and the women busied themselves preparing for a long day. Fru Gaino pointed out to me the possible site that might be the best for me to await them. She could not be sure, however, and it was left to me to decide for myself.

It was no easy decision. I had set out alone, with cameras and food for the day, and knew that I must succeed on this day if I really wanted to capture some of the excitement and the drama of this ancient act—this eternal play that has no ending, but rotates round the whole of the seasons year after year.

Soon I had climbed above the camp site, on which I could now look down, and fortunately the sun was behind me. There were so many times when I wished I could have moved with nothing in my hands . . . as it was, I always felt something like a pack animal, or perhaps as the Lapp dogs must have felt with the wooden clubs round their necks.

Carefully I studied each section of the rocks, mostly covered with heather and grass, but sometimes showing through as big grey masses where they were bare of vegetation.

Then, at last, at the top of a high, grey slope, came the moving figures. They were up there . . . or some of them at any rate.

Climbing upwards again, I reached a high point from which I had a fine view of the whole of the very lovely valley, lit by the sun, and showing a wide range of colours in the thick undergrowth.

There was no sound. The figures had disappeared into a dip, but suddenly, through the thick belt of birch trees that grew up the sides of a slope at the back of me the forms of the deer began to appear. Very small, like ants, they seemed at first, and my blood moved faster through my veins. I began to feel the thrill of it all in my scalp, which tingled. My fingers did not feel so steady, but I tried to control my excitement.

a lot depended on my own quietness at that moment, for I could so easily have scared the deer into a wrong direction.

Very soon the group I had first sighted came from the shelter of the trees and began to move, quietly and with a slow, steady grace, in a long line towards the round-up area. They were quite alone. No humans were guiding them. Instinct and the desire to resassemble into a herd was bringing them together just as it would have done if no Lapps had been present at all.

The old wild herds must have gathered together in a similar manner in bygone centuries, and it was impossible not to think of those earlier days as I began to watch what proved to be a sight of the greatest beauty and thrill. Quite unnoticed by the deer, I felt that I was the only human in the area, in the heart of an age-old pageant of movement.

From every point of the compass, or so it appeared to my mind at that moment, slow-moving columns of deer began to appear over the tops of the rocks, all gradually converging to one point.

What most marvellous luck to have chosen this spot! Right in front of me was a high ridge, along which column after column passed, with the sun shining directly upon their richly coloured coats. They made no sound whatever. It was as though I was watching a film, with the silence broken only by the sound of the crows overhead.

Then, right behind me, another bunched-up group appeared, among which were many quite lightly coloured calves. They saw me, stopped for a moment, then sprang off in a long fast-moving line in front of me and down the slope to the bottom of the valley. There they crossed a neck of the lake, and climbing up the other side of the rocks joined up with the main column again.

I was able to film this wonderful sight, to my great thrill and pleasure. Already I was thinking of the future and of how many youngsters in England would be able to learn something in their school lessons about this wild life through the eyes of my camera. It was a moving feeling, and to make the whole setting complete, at the rear of this group, far behind them, came the small figure of young Aslak, with his rucksack on his back and his dog by his side. He saw me, waved, and moved on, a perfect symbol of the part that the human played in this drama.

His young form, with the weather-beaten face, was soon lost to view as he disappeared over the rising rocks on the other side of the valley in the wake of the group of calves.

He signified the end of the columns of moving deer. I waited for a while longer, but the big herd had now passed, and I knew that they would already be assembling in the large enclosure that had been prepared for them.

Hastily, I began to make my way back along the trail. The sun was now very warm, warmer than I had felt it all summer, and it would be very hot and tired Lapp herders who would finish off this day, I felt.

I reached the last ridge and could see the camp and the fjord below me. The flat space which had been so bare when I left was now alive with a moving mass of reindeer. It was an inspiring sight. They did not appear to be in any hurry, but quietly spreading themselves out and soon filled the big area and began to eat.

The Lapp herders, who had been in the hills in search of them, had now assembled in a bunch at the end of the field, where the women already sat in a group.

A fire was soon lit among the heather, over which hung the black pot and into it were dropped pieces of freshly caught salmon that had been fished during the night from the lake high above.

The men sat around the fire, ill dressed, dirty, and unshaven, but full of life, and as I watched them eventually eat the salmon with great relish, washing this down with mugs of coffee, I had to agree that they were right when they said they would not change their life. The sheer health of it kept them without illness, and although they had had no sleep that night, they now had to prepare for a very hard day ahead.

As the smoke rose into the still and warm air the men joked, cutting huge chunks of bread with their knives, whilst the women and the young girls kept together in another group.

Around the fire were little Per Kemi, Mikkel Kemi, young Aslak, Per Sara, Ole Gaino and young Jesef Gaino, all eager to get on with the task ahead of them. But it was necessary to have a break after their long night, and they stretched out their legs and smoked for a short while.

Getting up, they shook themselves, pulled their belts a little tighter, and took their lassos from their shoulders. Ole Gaino came close to me, looked me straight in the eyes and smiled in his very friendly way.

This was a big day, and yet only the start of several, for the killing, sorting of the herd, marking of the ears, and castrating of selected bucks, would continue for some time, until all was clear, and the final slaughtered buck had been taken away by the eager buyers. There were no lack of businessmen ready to buy from the Lapps, for they can make a good profit, and by the time the reindeer steaks have reached such places as Oslo or Stockholm, then indeed their price has risen enormously. They even reach London, and I can certainly recommend that reindeer steaks be ordered if the chance arises. One can then at least travel in the imagination back to the old site in the north of Norway from which possibly they started their journey to your table.

The reindeer began to move . . . I knew the signs from the days of the spring crossing when we had tried to get them on to the 'pram'. As soon as the Lapp herders and the two boys started swinging their lassos among them, aiming for the antlers, the deer bunched together and began their big, swinging rotating movement. The men stood in the centre, whilst the herd milled round and round at an ever-faster pace. One after another the antlers were caught by a skilfully thrown lasso, and then the tussle between man and beast would begin.

A powerful reindeer in good condition is something indeed to have on the end of a line! It could easily pull the Lapp along, and it took two or three men to hold the end of the rope whilst they fought gradually to get nearer to the struggling beast.

The deer would put its head down and swing back violently from side to side, whilst all around the others still ran in circles. At last the men sprang at the antlers, and twisted the head on one side, so that the animal was forced over and on to the ground.

There, if it was a fine buck that needed castrating, it had to be held down by several Lapps whilst Mikkel, with his very strong teeth, performed the operation on the genitals. For centuries this had been the old method, and it needed just the right grip and knowledge to do it. Not every Lapp was fitted for the task, and usually as in this group, the young herder with the largest mouth and strongest grip with his teeth was given the job.

Mikkel now threw himself quickly down at the deer, and within a few moments it was all over. The buck was released, and after a moment of hesitation sprang up, and with eyes that shone with fear quickly ran back into the main body.

In my own excitement and eagerness to watch, a huge buck came very close to knocking me flying, for I stood right in its path as it jumped up after having been castrated. At the last second it swerved, however, or I would have felt the points of its fine antlers. I was now so filled with tense excitement that I had become almost hypnotized by the fast swinging rhythm of the whole performance.

Once again in the centre of the deer, which swung first one way and then suddenly changed direction, a Lapp jumped out with his lasso. I was gripped by the sight of the swaying mass of antlers, and also by the silence of the animals, except for their low grunts. The hoofs thundered over the rock and grass, but there was little other sound.

Per Kemi missed many times in his throwing, and I felt he was perhaps losing his skill. But he persuaded me to keep near him to watch how it was done, and when he did lasso a deer that looked as though it would have pulled him over the hills I jumped quickly to help him, as did several of the others. I watched his eyes light up with pleasure, and I felt that he indeed had enjoyed his life on the trail, and was determined not to give it up until he had to. I could imagine him throwing his lasso for many more years, and as I write this account he will be preparing soon for another spring migration, I am sure, as I left him in the best of health and humour.

The day began to be very hot. For the first time since summer started the north was showing us that it could also be warm when it wished. It seemed to have chosen a strange time, however, now that the autumn was here. The Lapps began to sweat freely, and soon clothing was being pulled off, and shirt-tails flying as they were pulled loose to give them more freedom of movement.

It was a heroic task in the heat, and soon they had to pause for long cooling drinks, and also for coffee. Coffee stimulates the Lapps as nothing else; it has the same effect upon them as a cup of tea seems to have on the English when they are tired. After it had been drunk there is a feeling of greater energy again, especially if much sugar is added, and the Lapps would pour a great deal of sugar, but no milk, into their drink.

The youngsters were very thrilled, for they were after their own calves, which they could throw and then have marked. Probably there can be no greater thrill in the life of the Lapp boy than this moment, when he is able to select his own calf for his lasso, and then know that it is his own for life.

Calf after calf, most of them with very pale coats, were thrown to the ground, and the ears cut quickly and expertly with the knife. They quickly sprang up, shook their heads, and then made off without a sound.

But castration, which was necessary so that the bucks could become tamer and of greater weight, was not the only reason the deer were being caught. For a large number of them this was their final hour. They were dragged to the edge of the field, and with a blow behind the ears, followed by a slit throat, they were silently killed. This was rather a difficult task for me to watch, as it was most unpleasant to see these fine beasts slaughtered in this way, with their heads held from the ground by their antlers, and blood running from their throats. But it was a necessary part of the Lapp life, for without this annual sale they could not live. The blood also had to be quickly drained to make the flesh better.

The animals were usually sold as they were, complete; although they could be skinned if required. There are today, I know, better and more efficient and more hygienic methods of killing and selling than that used by the Sara family, but we were far removed from any of the centres that have been set up for dealing with the carcasses, and this had always been their method. Whether they will be changed in the future only time will tell. There was, however, one sign of officialdom present; a young Norwegian, one of a force employed by the Government to keep their eye on such operations and to see that all went smoothly. He was a very helpful young man, who spent his time among the deer, assisting with the pulling and castrating.

The women kept away from all this, gathering at the end of the field, where they kept a supply of food and drink ready. However, one, Hannah, was right in the heart of all the operations. One could never keep her out of anything; she was a remarkable woman.

The day gradually passed and the sun threw long shadows over the ground. The milling herd was still being given no peace, for when the weather was as fine as this the herders wished to take advantage of it. But as evening came they at last dropped their lassos, returned to the camp, and they and the herd settled down for the night. A well-earned rest and hot meals for the Lapps, and quiet grazing for the deer.

It had, indeed, been one to the most exciting and stimulating days I had lived through, but I was haunted at night by the sight of the pools of red staining the grass. It had not been a bloodless day.

CHAPTER 19

The End of a Great Adventure

THE milling of the reindeer, the marking of the calves, castration
of the bucks, and the killing, continued for several days; after
which the herd would be ready for the start of the autumn
journey to the winter plain.

Hannah and I would not be taking part in this, however, for our
first loyalty was to our own group back at Altneset, and we would be
needed there.

A feeling of sadness crept over me when I thought how I, too, would
so soon have to make my own long return journey back to England,
in the wake of the migrating starlings.

The boat trip back to Altneset was again made at night. The next
day there was a real feel of autumn in the air and we decided to gather
another bag of the 'bleksoppa' mushrooms. First boiled, and then fried,
they were delicious.

That same evening, when the Lapps were having a small party of
their own, I was invited over to the Internat School. It would be a
treat for the young Norwegian teaching couple, I thought, if I took a
large number of the mushrooms to go with our meal, for I knew they
were frying reindeer steak. But they regarded my gift with great
suspicion, feeling sure they must be poisonous.

This was the first time for months that I had been able to relax in a
comfortable armchair in civilized surroundings. It was than that I
suddenly realized just how primitive my life had become from the
time, so long ago, when I had left Cambridge. How amazingly the

human can adapt, though. Every night I had slept on a pile of reindeer skins, but I would not have changed them for a comfortable bed in this apartment. They had become as much a part of my life as the berries, the fish, the crow, and the Lapps themselves.

The couple were immensely interested in all my adventures. They had very little knowledge themselves of Lapp ways, and, of course, unless one has lived with them, the Lapp life is hardly known in any detail whatever, even by the Norwegians.

We finished our evening with wine, and music from their large radio. But as soon as I climbed the rocky path in the darkness and the wind towards my old hut I was back again in the primitive world, where only the crow greeted me with a low croak. The smell of smoke and reindeer skins assailed my nostrils. I had become now so used to these smells that I had not realized how they had permeated all my clothing. The Norwegian couple had pointed this out to me, as politely as possible; I must have smelled like any of the nomads to them.

Next morning in spite of a bright sun, there was a cold wind blowing hard. A sense of isolation gripped me and I could well imagine how bleak the oncoming winter would be; particularly when they told me that my hut would soon be so deep under snow that only the long stove pipe would show above the surface.

There were several days for me now to spend alone, as Hannah and some of the Sara Lapps were away on the other side of the fjord, preparing for the gathering together of their herd. This would take some time, and then the deer would swim back to our side of the bay. All depended on the weather, however, for the animals disliked strong winds and swift currents, so the Lapps would have to wait for a calm day.

One evening after a long day's lone expedition, I returned to my hut, and as I reached the door I had a sinking feeling in my stomach . . . the lock hung broken, and the door swung open.

The crow flew out to greet me. I managed to find and light the small oil lamp and, gazing round the hut, I expected to see that my valuables had been stolen. But my cameras still hung on the walls, and nothing seemed to have been taken. My eyes travelled round until they came to the place on a side box where the large can of home-brewed beer I had left fermenting had been standing. It had disappeared. The explanation of the break-in was apparent. The intruders had been interested in only one thing—the drink that they must have known was there.

My indignation at this intrusion was great, but it was mixed with much thankfulness that my equipment was all intact. That was, in fact, all that mattered. I imagined it had been some passing herders and I did not begrudge the Lapps the beer. They would have thought nothing of breaking my lock. To them the locked door was a sign of inhospitality, and I should have left it open!

The following morning was again bright and filled with a quiet, almost waiting, calmness. There was the same feeling that one senses before a big storm.

It was on this day that Nils had decided to take me with him to visit the oldest of all the nomads, the 'Grandfather' of the big Sara family, old Mikkel Matis. Although he was then eighty-five or more he was still keeping his isolated watch on the deer at the end of the lonely and dramatic Bekkafjord. In a small rough tent, made of birch branches, around which he had pulled an old piece of dark green sailcloth, he had been manning this far-away outpost, on his own, until the autumn swim of the deer.

Along the fjord, with its tranquil water, we passed other Lapps in small boats, with fencing and poles, preparing for their own autumn gatherings of their herds. High up on the immense dark grey rocks on either side of the water we could see at times tiny figures silhouetted. These were Lapp herders, all on the task of rounding up, and anxious that not one of their reindeer should be left behind if they could help it. It was a time of great activity everywhere, for the autumn was now reaching its climax, and we could expect the big storms to hit us at almost any moment.

After three of four hours we reached the end of the fjord and left the boat. Amid the yellowing leaves of the birch trees high above us we could see the small green tentcloth, and a thin rising column of smoke. We had found Mikkel Matis.

We reached him after a stiff climb and he was most glad to see us, for I was amazed to see that he appeared to have absolutely nothing in the way of food or any comforts at all in the tent.

His old stubble-covered face, with eyes bleary from the smoke of so many fires, broke into a wide smile when he saw us; and as he sat contentedly in the tent's opening, smoking his huge old pipe while Nils rekindled the dead ashes and soon had water boiling in the battered oll iron pot. Mikkel watched with great interest to see what we had brought, for his first thoughts were for tobacco. He was also more than ready for food.

There he sat, clothed as only a real Lapp of the old nomads can be, with his aged skin leggings, dirty and stained blouse, his hat pulled down over his forehead, and his cloak of fur. He had nothing but a skin to sleep on, and was a living example of the healthiness of the trail life, and the power of attraction that it has over such people.

It was his task to guard this flank and to guide the deer away from this point of the fjord. He was quite alone, and yet, at this advanced age, he was determined not to give up the life.

We eventually left him, standing there alone, in the fading light, puffing his pipe. His squat bent-kneed figure looked forlorn between the golden-yellow of the birch saplings; but I knew that he was a happy man, as he had himself told me. He had been most pleased to see an Englishman, and had recounted to me in a Norwegian dialect that was very difficult for me to follow something of his own long life, which, like that of old Fru Sara, had been spent moving backwards and forwards, spring and autumn, year after year.

As I looked at Nils Sara, rowing quietly along the fjord, in the late evening light, I was sure he would grow into a second Mikkel Matis; he was of exactly the same mould, and full of admiration for the old man. He paused and let his oars rest and we felt the full ageless majesty of the fjord. Even he, used to the life as he was, was keenly aware of the beauty around him. Although he was as tough and leathery as could be, he had a very sensitive nature, which might have been surprising had I not learned something of the Lapp way of thinking and of their old religious beliefs.

He now wanted to show me, even in this gloom, the place of an old Lapp worshipping rock or *Seide*, way above us on the crags. So we climbed up and were just able to see, in the deep luminous twilight, how nature itself had fashioned this strange almost human-faced rock. It stood there with several stones and old reindeer antlers arranged in a half-circle around it. This, then, had been an old worshipping place for the herders who passed this way. Here they had approached on their knees and begged for good fortune for the reindeer and themselves. As the wind sighed around us, on this lonely evening, in the autumn of the north, and the leaves rustled restlessly, I could well understand how this rock had impressed itself upon the Lapps as a supernatural symbol.

Nils stood silent, as we both gazed, lost in our own thoughts.

The splash of the oars sounded with great clarity in the still air as we neared our camp site, several hours later. A light from the window in Nils's family hut showed like a welcoming yellow beacon. As always, it was good to be back again.

Friday, the first of October . . . I knew that the calm could not last much longer, and sure enough it did not.

On this day the wind swept down quite suddenly from the hills with a dramatic whining fury, bringing with it the first of the autumn snow. From the heights surrounding us the snow was scattered in a misty layer over the rich colour of the vegetation under our feet, and the yellow and red leaves showered down from the trees in their thousands.

My ramshackle hut, built only of driftwood and railway sleepers washed up from the fjord, began to shake. Then the sides bent inwards with the full force of the autumn gale, and soon it was impossible to see through the small windows because of the driving snow that smacked against them. Fortunately we had been expecting this and I had chopped up a good supply of firewood beforehand.

Hannah, who had now returned, took it all calmly. She started to make pancakes on the old stove, saying it was their custom on the first day of the snow. Everything shook violently and the flames roared through the cracks in the old broken-down stove, most dangerously. But customs must be adhered to! The snow was beginning to seep through small holes in the roof and drip on to the stove, where it sizzled and quickly dried. We were not warm by any means, but I was glad of the hours that I had spent at odd times during the summer making the hut a little more weatherproof.

All that day and night the blizzard continued. When it died, and we looked around us, there was desolation everywhere. Almost every leaf had been stripped from the trees, which now stood in naked rows again, for another bare icy winter. The reign of the snow had returned and it was as though the splendid, brilliant autumn had never been. I had been warned that this would happen, but the very suddenness and immense change of scenery is something hard to describe. It is part of the surprising and dramatic character of the north.

This was a hard time for the Sara herders. They were all sheltering as best they could on the slopes opposite. The big herd had to be somehow brought down in a solid mass to the one spot on our side, which was their traditional point for swimming across the small bay. It needed good calm weather for this swim, which could easily go wrong. The men had worked very hard searching for their small groups of deer amongst the rocks and over the heights, where they had wandered so freely all the summer, and this big storm had hindered them greatly. Reindeer always dislike storms and will scatter quickly in such conditions. This is what the herders had feared and why they had been trying to gather them together before the fury broke.

Anxiously we searched through our binoculars for signs of men or beasts, but the visibility was very poor and heavy mist shrouded round the slopes.

With great good fortune the next day was calm and the sun lit up the water once more. Immediately there was great activity among the whole family. At last through our binoculars we saw a long, thin column of about six hundred deer descending the blue grey slopes, now patched with snow.

This was the sight we had waited a long time to see. Everyone went along a narrow path to the water's side where the deer would land, and where they would remain overnight. A grey haze began to settle over the mountains, making the valley gloomy and the light poor; but the weather was calm with no wind, and this was the important thing. Nils now rowed over and the herd began to gather at the edge of the water on the other side of the bay. Then he fixed the leading reindeer by a long rope to his boat, and began to pull again. The deer plunged in, dragged by the boat, and the herd started to follow. One by one they jumped into the clear water, and soon there was a long line of beasts swimming over with antlers held high. On either flank the Lapp herders in their boats, prevented the deer turning to one side or the other and returning to the slopes of their summer pastures. We on our side had to remain quiet and calm; any sudden loud noise would have been fatal, for the deer easily panic when they are swimming to land in this way.

All went well, and Nils landed, with the first deer rising from the water beside him. One after another they emerged, shook themselves very vigorously, and gathered together among the vegetation and

The End of a Great Adventure 191

rocks that made a natural corral at the base of the cliffs. Enclosed as it was, the Lapps had little difficulty in keeping the herd under control. Nils and Aslak had to return to the other side, however, for they knew even without counting that they were still some deer short, and all must be found.

The huge herd milled round and round for a time, then began to settle. Old Fru Sara, completely in charge of the operation, moved among the herders; there was an authority about her that none dared disobey, as, still straight of back, she walked at the head of her own regal beast, directing with her stick. Despite her age, the men did not argue with her in this vital matter, and the women also quickly did what they were told. Hannah and she sat together on a high rock in the heart of the mêlée, from where they could control the whole scene, and very soon, in the gathering gloom of the afternoon, there was order. The deer ate contentedly, and those who were to watch over them for the night donned their thick fur cloaks and started their long period of waiting.

Berit, Hannah and Fru Sara pulled their bright red plaid shawls tighter round their shoulders, and sat by the smoky fire in the open. They had had another tiring day, and in the damp blanket of cold they were glad to brew up the inevitable strong coffee. The dogs, who had been restrained all day, stretched themselves and settled down happily to sleep.

Under the clear sky the stars shone with a quiet piercing brilliance. The herders would have to remain to keep the herd intact, but the rest of us returned to our huts.

The cycle was now almost complete. The deer next day would start to be driven back, over the two hundred or so miles of hills, rivers and tundra. Back to the small far-away group of wooden huts at Gargosletten in the heart of the great Finnmark plain, just as they had been for centuries. The gigantic white desert of snow covering this plain in winter has a silence so complete that in the luminous half-darkness of midday even the blood pulsating through ones veins sounds like a rushing river in the ears.

Around the frozen lake, by the side of which the Sara family have their temporary winter encampment, the herd would wander freely. Watched over by a herder and his dogs, they would dig once more for the reindeer moss to keep them alive until next April. Then they would return again to these slopes on the coast, which are so rich in food, for the summer months.

The rutting season is from late September to early November, and the men were anxious now that they should move quickly to the grounds where traditionally the herd had always rested on the way, during this mating period. They would be late this year, for the weather had held them up, and were therefore restless and the bucks eager to fight.

For me, too, this was a moment of parting, and also of great sadness, for it was now that I had to finally take leave of these ancient and courageous people of whom I had become so fond. The next day I was due to take the fjord steamer to Hammerfest, from where I should begin the long coastal journey back to Bergen.

Did I really want to return to civilization? My heart knew that I did not. For a while I had been privileged to be a part of a free, uncomplicated but hard way of life, amongst a kind, self-reliant and unspoilt people, whose culture has survived even in this modern age. I knew it would affect the whole of my future thinking.

The pack animals had been loaded with all they could carry; skin bags were slung from either side; all was ready for the departure.

My farewells had been said, unemotionally, for such is the Lapp custom. Then in the early hours of a very bitter grey morning the whole contingent moved off and were quickly enveloped, like phantoms, in the mist.

Sadly I took my own possessions down to the end of the small pier. It was bitingly cold, as the snow came swirling along the fjord.

I waved to a small group on the pier as the steamer drew away; then the village began to recede into snowy distance, and was soon lost to sight. As I went down into the warmth of the cabin I felt a heaviness of depression settle over me. However, I had refused to part with one friend, and in a hastily made wooden box by my side sat Charlie the crow, my faithful companion, who returned all the way to England with me as a living reminder of my part in the age-old pageant of the nomadic Lapps.